COLLEGE STUDY

The Essential Ingredients

SALLY LIPSKY

INDIANA UNIVERSITY OF PENNSYLVANIA

PEARSON

Prentice
Hall

Upper Saddle River, New Jersey
Columbus, Ohio

Library of Congress Cataloging-in-Publication Data

Lipsky, Sally.
    College study : the essential ingredients / Sally Lipsky.
       p. cm.
    Includes index.
    ISBN 0-13-048836-4
    1. Study skills. 2. Critical thinking—Studying and teaching (Higher) 3. College student
orientation. I. Title.

  LB2395.L49 2004
  378.1'0281—dc21   2003051762

Vice President and Executive Publisher: Jeffery W. Johnston
Senior Acquisitions Editor: Sande Johnson
Assistant Editor: Cecilia Johnson
Editorial Assistant: Erin Anderson
Production Editor: Holcomb Hathaway
Design Coordinator: Diane C. Lorenzo
Cover Designer: Jason Moore
Cover Photos: Hemera Technologies, Inc.
Production Manager: Pamela D. Bennett
Director of Marketing: Ann Castel Davis
Director of Advertising: Kevin Flanagan
Marketing Manager: Christina Quadhamer
Compositor: Aerocraft Charter Art Service
Cover Printer: Coral Graphic Services, Inc.
Printer/Binder: R. R. Donnelley & Sons Company

> ### DEDICATION
>
> *In loving memory of Merle.*
> *In loving gratitude to Rick,*
> *Jennie, and Kylie.*

Pearson Education Ltd.
Pearson Education Singapore Pte. Ltd.
Pearson Education Canada, Ltd.
Pearson Education–Japan

Pearson Education Australia Pty. Limited
Pearson Education North Asia Ltd.
Pearson Educación de Mexico, S.A. de C.V.
Pearson Education Malaysia Pte. Ltd.

10 9 8 7 6 5 4 3 2 1
ISBN 0-13-048836-4

CHAPTER 1	CHAPTER 2	CHAPTER 3	CHAPTER 4	CHAPTER 5	CHAPTER 6	CHAPTER 7	CHAPTER 8
Academic Success	Managing Time	Study Environment	Active Listening	Reading Textbooks	Enhancing Memory	Test Success	Continuing Success

BRIEF CONTENTS

C O N T E N T S

Chapter 3

CONTROLLING YOUR STUDY ENVIRONMENT   37

Chapter 4

ACTIVE LISTENING AND NOTE TAKING   49

Chapter 5

Chapter 6

Chapter 7

Chapter 8

Appendix

P R E F A C E

This text contains a complete and balanced coverage of essential learning and study techniques, with an emphasis on critical thinking at the college level. Readers are exposed to *how* to learn, while understanding *why* they learn, within the context of making informed choices about strategies that work best for them. After immediate transfer of a specific learning strategy into daily academic life, students critique its effectiveness. Content is presented in such a way as to guide students to become self-regulating learners and problem solvers.

Features

The text integrates three separate yet interrelated elements of how students learn:

1. *Strategies.* The text covers important and practical study techniques that students can apply immediately in their daily academic courses.
2. *Attitude.* The text provides opportunities for students to explore their levels of interest, motivation, and commitment to transferring learning techniques in their day-to-day lives as college students.
3. *Learning styles.* Individual differences in learning preferences and tendencies can help students successfully implement learning and study strategies. As such, readers become aware of and apply techniques that match *how they learn best.* Two models of learning styles are presented in the text: (1) use of the Myers-Briggs Type Indicator® inventory to determine learning preferences, and (2) use of visual, auditory, and tactile/kinesthetic dimensions of learning.

Additional features of the text include:

- A streamlined format and an informal, personal writing style that maintain the *reader's attention.*
- A focus on *modeling* the essentials of learning so that readers can readily transfer strategies to content course work. Illustrations of how peers apply specific strategies, in the form of visual examples and students' comments, provide appealing, convincing models.
- Relevant activities designed to immediately *engage* readers.
- An appendix linking results of the Learning and Study Strategies Inventory (LASSI) with text chapters. The LASSI is a self-report instrument that assesses college students' use of and attitudes toward learning and study strategies, as defined by 10 scales: attitude, motivation, time management, anxiety, concentration, information processing, selecting main ideas, study aids, self-testing, and test strategies. As described in the appendix, each of the 10 scales in the LASSI correlates with topics presented in *College Study: The Essential Ingredients.*

This text is intended for use in either a two-year or four-year institution within a variety of contexts:

- A study skills or learning strategies course (likely one or two credits)
- A skills course "linked" or "paired" with content-area course work
- An introductory-level content course using a supplemental learning strategies text
- A first-year orientation program or seminar
- A series of workshops for first-year students
- A peer educator training course requiring a college learning strategies text

Furthermore, an *Instructor's Manual* accompanies the text and includes:

- Suggestions for how to use *text features* for in-class activities, including small-group work, collaborative work, journal writing, and group discussion.
- *Problem-solving scenarios* centered on topics presented in the text chapters. These scenarios lend themselves to in-class group work that reinforces decision-making skills.
- Five-point *chapter quizzes* that provide a modest check of students' comprehension. Instructors may choose to use the quizzes as an extrinsic incentive for students to read assigned chapters.
- A sample *syllabus,* including an outline of activities for a one-credit or two-credit college learning skills course.

Acknowledgments

We would like to thank the following reviewers for their constructive comments for the improvement of this book: Terri Bruce, Kellogg Community College; Renee Bugenhagen, Medaille College; Norma Jean Campbell, Fayetteville State University; James C. Cebulski, University of South Florida; Jacek Dalecki, Indiana University; Robin Diana, Rochester Institute of Technology; Anthony R. Easley, Valencia Community College; Jane Eddy, Viterbo University; Kathleen A. Hoag, Michigan State University; Janet Keen, University of Texas at Arlington; Kim Long, Valencia Community College; Paul E. Panek, The Ohio State University–Newark; and Cathy Pearson, Kent State University.

To the Student:
An Introduction to Text Features

At the Beginning of Chapters

Focus questions. Examine the "Focus Questions" when previewing the chapter. Then read to discover the answers to the questions. This strategy will help you become a more perceptive, involved reader.

Chapter terms. These are key vocabulary terms introduced in the chapter. Before beginning to read, review the terms. Then, when you have completed the chapter, check your understanding by providing both a meaning and an example for each term.

Within Chapters

Pause . . . and reflect. These exercises provide opportunities to think about and process key ideas. Questions guide the direction of your observations and commentary. Your instructor might ask you and your classmates to share reflections as part of group discussion or activities.

Models. These are examples illustrating how other college students applied strategies in a variety of courses. Use these models as templates for your own course work.

Student voices. Interspersed within chapters are compelling comments from other college students. Reading about your peers' experiences and suggestions can help to guide and motivate you to apply similar strategies.

"My first impression of this study skills course was that it is a 'blow-off' class, but my attitude has changed tremendously. I've really learned a lot during these past weeks, a lot more than I thought I would. I've been applying much of the knowledge and the methods in my other classes, and it's working. So far this semester my grades are good, and I think this course has a lot to do with it. Finally, I am achieving the goals that I set a long time ago and, as a result, feel much better about myself as a student." —SEAN

"I entered college feeling motivated; however, unsuccessful attempts in my classes left me feeling drained. Overall, I came into this course feeling down on myself, a failure, but I am leaving a new person. Topics covered in the course helped me a great deal (even if it was just a review for some topics). Currently, I enjoy knowing that I can accomplish college-level courses. The results of this class are enduringly rewarding." —MARTA

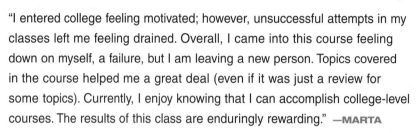

try it out!

These exercises direct you to immediately *apply* a strategy introduced in that chapter, a crucial aspect of developing a personal system of study.

At the End of Chapters

Personal Action Statements. You will choose specific strategies to implement within a designated time frame. After implementing your Personal Action Statements, you will **Assess Your Success** with the purpose of identifying what techniques do and do not work for you. Through this process—choosing, using, and assessing strategies—you will work toward building an effective, efficient study system for yourself.

Chapter conclusions provide a practical overview of the essential strategies. They also are a useful reference for future semesters.

CHAPTER 1	CHAPTER 2	CHAPTER 3	CHAPTER 4	CHAPTER 5	CHAPTER 6	CHAPTER 7	CHAPTER 8
Academic Success	Managing Time	Study Environment	Active Listening	Reading Textbooks	Enhancing Memory	Test Success	Continuing Success

CHAPTER 1

Creating Academic Success

FOCUS QUESTIONS

What are the three essential ingredients of a system of study?

Why is each important?

How am I going to apply each?

CHAPTER TERMS

After reading this chapter, define (in your own words) and provide an example for each of the following terms:

- active learning behaviors
- extrinsic reward
- intrinsic reward
- learning style
- passive learning behaviors
- Personal Action Statement

A System of Study: The Essential Ingredients

As a college student, you no doubt have experienced—or will experience—approaches toward instruction and requirements for learning unlike in your previous years of education. Recent high school graduates often welcome the greater personal and social freedoms associated with college life. However, along with these freedoms come the challenges associated with the greater academic and personal responsibilities of college life. No longer does a teacher or a parent oversee your learning; at the postsecondary level, you, the student, are expected to be a self-directed and self-motivated learner.

For the nontraditional student, college life offers a different set of challenges: returning to school after a hiatus often creates a complicated juggling act among job, family, and academic responsibilities. Whatever the personal circumstances, individual students require their own set of learning strategies to effectively meet the multifaceted challenges encountered at the college level. The purpose of this text is to provide you, the student, with the tools for developing these strategies so that you become a self-directed learner and are able to achieve academic success throughout your college career.

By the time you enter college, you have developed a system of study that is based upon three essential ingredients:

1. Your learning behaviors
2. Your learning attitudes
3. Your learning style

Each of these is discussed in the following sections.

Your Learning Behaviors

The term *learning behaviors* refers to a variety of actions done in an academic situation. These learning behaviors combine to form your system of study. Note that some behaviors are conducive to learning, such as arriving at class several minutes early with notepaper and pen, sitting in the front or middle of a classroom, listening attentively and selectively, asking questions to clarify points, reviewing notes after class, seeking out help when needed, and so on. These are termed **active learning behaviors** because they represent self-responsibility, initiative, and involvement in the learning process. Active learning behaviors lead to successful outcomes—that is, high grades and a smooth path toward graduation.

On the other hand, many behaviors can impede learning, such as skipping classes, sleeping during class, yielding to distractions, studying after social and leisure activities, and not seeking assistance. These are termed **passive learning behaviors.** Students exhibiting these behaviors do *not* take charge of their learning. Passive learners often are not accustomed to working hard in school; they tend to exert minimal time and effort in their academic lives.

The purpose of this text is to introduce you to active learning behaviors at the college level. Each chapter focuses on a group of active learning behaviors— or strategies—related to a major study skills topic. Principal elements of each topic are labeled "Essential Ingredients." Within each chapter you will be given choices of which behaviors, or strategies, you will put into practice as you engage in your day-to-day college course work.

Your Learning Attitudes

Your attitude toward all aspects of academic life (going to class, interacting with the instructors, completing assignments, studying) has a huge impact on your accomplishments in college. Successful college students exhibit the following characteristics:

- **Motivation**—They *want* to achieve and are determined to reach their academic goals.
- **Persistence**—They do not let hurdles block personal achievement. When problems arise, they seek out help and persevere until a satisfactory solution is reached.
- **Self-discipline**—They are willing to make the necessary sacrifices and devote the necessary efforts toward receiving that college degree.
- **A personal support network**—They have at least one family member or close friend whom they can rely on for personal encouragement and support. Likewise, they tend to associate with peers who are responsible and caring.

How many of these characteristics do you exhibit at this point in your college career? As you read the upcoming chapters in this text, you will be exploring your outlook toward the many aspects of college life and determining if your attitudes work *for* or *against* your immediate and long-term successes. In college, *you* will be determining your own academic path; thus it is up to you to take responsibility for your successes—or failures. This mission of self-determination and responsibility can be accomplished by an awareness of *why* you are here, *what* you want to accomplish, and *how* you can develop a viewpoint that contributes to personal success.

pause... *and reflect*

- What motivates you to achieve?
- Are you persistent when faced with a problem or stumbling block? Provide a personal example.
- Would you describe yourself as being self-disciplined in regard to school? In what areas are you self-disciplined? In what areas are you not self-disciplined; explain *why*.
- Who is part of your personal support network?

Your Learning Style

Your learning behaviors and attitudes are, to some degree, shaped by what is termed your **learning style.** Learning styles are preferences in behaviors that are characteristic of each person, that is, *how a person learns best*. For instance, one student prefers variety and action and therefore joins a study group for subjects. Another student prefers a quiet study environment and works alone contentedly. This student chooses to study at a carrel tucked away in an upper floor of the campus library. Both students are just as effective with their studying, yet both follow differing paths as to *how* they study. This is part of the individual preferences, or learning style, that they have developed throughout the years. By assessing and analyzing your learning style, you can create a system of study that is both comfortable and successful for you.

MYERS-BRIGGS TYPE INDICATOR®*

Numerous instruments are available for identifying learning style. The Myers-Briggs Type Indicator® (MBTI®) personality inventory (Briggs & Myers, 1998) is a widely used, standardized instrument for assessing personality "types," or preferences, based on the work of Swiss psychologist Carl Jung. The MBTI® inventory identifies personality types according to four dichotomies:

- Extraversion (E) or Introversion (I)
- Sensing (S) or Intuition (N)
- Thinking (T) or Feeling (F)
- Judging (J) or Perceiving (P)

Throughout this book, these four dichotomies are used in exercises in which you will be matching your learning *style* with specific learning *strategies*. If you do *not* have access to the MBTI® instrument, you can obtain an immediate estimate of your learning preferences by completing the following informal exercise (Lawrence, 1993, pp. 2–4).

*MBTI, Myers-Briggs, and Myers-Briggs Type Indicator are trademarks or registered trademarks of the Myers-Briggs Type Indicator Trust in the United States and other countries.

try it out!

Assessing Your Learning Style

Directions: Read the two preferences in each row. In a **learning situation**—that is, when you are *listening* to a lecture, *reading* a book, *concentrating* on homework, *writing* a paper, or *preparing* for a test—which **one** of the two characteristics describes you **most of the time?** Put a "✓" in that circle.

SCALE I	
Extraversion *OR*	**Introversion**

Extraversion	Introversion
○ I prefer action and variety. things.	○ I prefer quiet and time to consider
○ I prefer talking to people when doing mental work.	○ I prefer to do mental work privately before talking.
○ I often act quickly, sometimes with little reflection.	○ I prefer to understand something *before* trying it.
○ I prefer to see how others do a task and to see results.	○ I prefer to understand the *idea* of a task and to work alone or with just a few people.
○ I want to know what other people expect of me.	○ I prefer setting my own standards.

Total number of "✓'s" for E _____   Total number of "✓'s" for I _____

SCALE II	
Sensing *OR*	**Intuition**

Sensing	Intuition
○ I usually pay most attention to *experience* and what something *is.*	○ I usually pay most attention to the *meanings* of facts and how they *fit together.*
○ I prefer to use my *senses*—see, hear, say, touch, smell—to find out what is happening.	○ I prefer to use my *imagination* to come up with different ways and possibilities to do things.
○ I dislike new problems *unless* I've had prior experiences regarding how to solve them.	○ I like solving *new* problems. I dislike doing the same thing over and over.
○ I enjoy *using skills already learned* more than learning new skills.	○ I enjoy *learning new skills* more than practicing old skills.
○ I am *patient with details,* but impatient when the details become complicated.	○ I am *impatient with details* and don't mind complicated situations.

Total number of "✓'s" for S _____   Total number of "✓'s" for N _____

SCALE III		
Thinking	*OR*	**Feeling**

○ I prefer to use *logic* when making decisions.	○ I prefer to use *personal feelings and values* when making decisions.
○ I expect to be treated with *justice and fairness.*	○ I expect praise and like to *please other people,* even in small matters.
○ I may neglect and hurt other people's feelings *without realizing it.*	○ I am usually very aware of *other people's feelings.*
○ I can get along with *little or no harmony* among people.	○ I feel unsettled by arguments and conflicts; I prefer *harmony* among people.
○ I tend to give more attention to *ideas or things,* rather than to human relationships.	○ I often can predict how others will *feel.*
Total number of "✓'s" for T _____	Total number of "✓'s" for F _____

SCALE IV		
Judging	*OR*	**Perceiving**

○ I prefer to make a *plan* and to have things settled and decided ahead of time.	○ I prefer to stay *flexible* and avoid fixed plans.
○ I prefer to make things come out the way they *ought to be.*	○ I deal easily with *unplanned and unexpected* happenings.
○ I prefer to *finish* one project before starting another.	○ I prefer to start many projects, though I may have *trouble completing* all of them.
○ I usually have my *mind made up* and may decide things too quickly.	○ I usually am seeking *new information* and may decide things too slowly.
○ I live by *standards and schedules* that are not easily changed.	○ I live by *making changes* to deal with problems as they come along.
Total number of "✓'s" for J _____	Total number of "✓'s" for P _____

Scoring: For Scales I–IV, total the number of "✓'s" in each column. Write the totals next to each preference.

PREFERENCES

SCALE I: _____ Extraversion (E) *or* _____ Introversion (I)

SCALE II: _____ Sensing (S) *or* _____ Intuition (N)

SCALE III: _____ Thinking (T) *or* _____ Feeling (F)

SCALE IV: _____ Judging (J) *or* _____ Perceiving (P)

Your dominant, clearer preference is the higher of the two numbers for each scale. Circle the term with the higher number for Scales I–IV; then write the four letters representing your "type" (for example, "ESFP" or "ISFJ"): _____

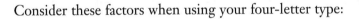

Source: People Types and Tiger Stripes, 3rd edition, by Gordon D. Lawrence. Center for Applications of Psychological Type, Gainesville, FL, 1993. Used with permission. This exercise is NOT a type indicator, not does it replicate the Myers-Briggs Type Indicator® which is a validated instrument.

Consider these factors when using your four-letter type:

1. **The higher the number, the more dominant or clearer is the preference.** For example, Anne has a total of 5 for the *Introvert* preference and Maria has a total of 3 for the *Introvert* preference. Though both are considered to be "introverted types," Anne likely exhibits clearer characteristics and preferences of an introverted personality.

2. **If the difference between the two numbers is slight—that is, only 1 point—then you may have no clear-cut dominant type for that scale.** For example, for SCALE III, Rob has a total of 3 for the *Thinking* preference and a total of 2 for the *Feeling* preference. He identifies *Thinking* as his prevailing preference; however, he likely also possesses many of the characteristics of the *Feeling* preference.

3. **By completing this informal exercise, you are receiving an *approximate* measure of your learning preferences.** (The standardized version of the Myers-Briggs Type Indicator® personality inventory is a much more reliable and valid measure of your preferences.)

At the end of select text chapters, you will be directed to identify, implement, and evaluate specific learning and study strategies that "match" your learning preferences or style.

VISUAL, AUDITORY, TACTILE/KINESTHETIC LEARNING STYLES

Another way to define learning style is by determining one's preference for visual, auditory, or tactile/kinesthetic modes of learning. Here is more information about each of those styles.

- **Visual learners** rely on spatial images when learning—that is, they learn best when they can "see" information in their mind. Visual learners often are proficient at identifying relationships among objects and ideas. When learning, they prefer illustrations and graphic formats, including the use of color and design.

- **Auditory learners** learn best when they "hear" information; thus, they tend to be proficient at listening, verbalizing, and discussing new knowledge. When learning information, auditory learners prefer to listen to tapes or CDs and to talk aloud, to themselves or with others.

- **Tactile/kinesthetic learners** rely on bodily awareness and sensory feelings when learning. "Tactile" refers to the use of *touch*, that is, the preference for manipulating tangible, concrete objects and materials when learning. "Kinesthetic" refers to *bodily* movement, that is, the preference for physical activity (moving about, dramatizing, going to labs or field trips) when learning.

Although you probably use all three modes of learning at various times and in varying situations, you most likely have a *dominant*, or *preferred*, means of learning. Because of the ease and popularity of defining learning style by way of *visual*, *auditory*, and *tactile/kinesthetic* dimensions, these three designations are included in upcoming chapter sections linking specific strategies with learning styles.

As you transfer suggested learning strategies to your daily course work, you will continually assess the success or failure of the strategies. The following section describes a process to assist you with applying and assessing strategies as you build and strengthen an effective system of study throughout your college career.

pause.... *and reflect*

What are the characteristics of your learning style? Describe *how you learn best* in each of these situations:

- You are reading a novel for English class.
- You are writing the first draft of a research paper.
- You are completing math homework problems.
- You are studying for a test in a science course.

A Path to Success: Personal Action Statements

A successful system of study requires much trial and error; you must *try* a strategy in order to know whether it will work for you. Your academic path in college will be strewn with both successes and failures. Savvy students are alert to what strategies *do* and *do not* work for them and, when needed, take the initiative to substitute other techniques. A **Personal Action Statement** is one way to oversee the piece-by-piece construction of your overall system of study. It is a concise, step-by-step, written plan of one specific strategy—either a behavior or an attitude—that you commit yourself to do within a predetermined span of time.

try it out!

Creating Your Personal Action Statement

Guidelines. Use these guidelines to ensure a successful Personal Action Statement.

1. Recognize that a Personal Action Statement is a *commitment to yourself* for action.

2. Make the Personal Action Statement manageable by identifying a *specific* step to implement.

3. Be realistic and honest with yourself. Identify a step, or strategy, that you *intend* to do, as well as hurdles and rewards for yourself.

4. Be willing to put both *thought* and *time* into the Personal Action Statement. Know that, for most students, the results are worth the effort. In little time, you will become adept at identifying and outlining strategies and steps. You will be able to see how the Personal Action Statements can *motivate* you toward action and achievement as you continue to build a system of study for yourself.

Format. The setup for the Personal Action Statement is:

1. I will: _____

_____

2. My greatest hurdle to achieving this is: _____

_____

3. I will eliminate this hurdle by: _____

_____

4. My time frame for achieving this is: _____

_____

5. My reward for achieving this is: _____

_____

On the *first line*, write what you intend to do. Write a strategy that is specific, realistic, and meaningful to you. Examples are:

- "I will study in a library study room three nights next week."
- "I will improve my concentration by taking short breaks every 30 minutes when reading my biology textbook."

The *second line* refers to what you anticipate to be the greatest barrier to completing the Personal Action Statement. Relying on past experiences and your personal weaknesses, what tends to hinder successful completion of your schoolwork? Examples of hurdles are boredom, the temptation to turn on your computer games, friends dropping by to chat, and your dislike of the subject matter or the instructor. Be honest with yourself—what tends to obstruct your study plans?

On the *third line*, write *how* you will overcome the hurdle identified in line two. What can you realistically do to reduce, if not eliminate, this barrier? For instance: you can study with a classmate to relieve boredom, or leave your computer games at home, or be more assertive with your friends, or talk to your professor about your problems.

On the *fourth line*, indicate your time frame. When are you going to implement this Personal Action Statement? Make the time frame immediate; begin as soon as possible.

On the *fifth line*, identify a reward for successfully completing your Personal Action Statement. Your reward can be **intrinsic** (such as a sense of satisfaction with a high test grade or increased confidence from knowing the subject matter) or **extrinsic** (such as watching a favorite television program, talking on the phone to a friend, or buying an ice cream cone).

After completing the Personal Action Statement, place it in an accessible location (such as above your desk or in your planner) so that you can refer to it regularly to remind yourself about your intentions.

The last, yet very important, step in this process is the *follow-up*. After you have implemented your Personal Action Statement, assess what happened. Did you accomplish all that you set out to accomplish? If so, great—reward yourself! Think about the factors that contributed to your success. Use the follow-up as a time to evaluate what happened and anticipate building on your successes.

Also, learn from your partial successes as well as your failures. If everything did not work out as anticipated, do not berate yourself. Keep in mind that risk taking is an inherent part of change, and it is inevitable that you will not always be successful when taking risks. However, do learn from your ineffective Personal Action Statements. Analyze what happened. Often students make their

Personal Action Statements either too general or too unrealistic (refer to the examples below). Examine how you can shape your Personal Action Statement to make it more specific and/or practical.

Examples of Personal Action Statements

TOO GENERAL:

I will improve my time management.

MORE SPECIFIC:

I will write class assignments in my planner.

TOO UNREALISTIC:

I will study in the library for three hours *every night* this week.

MORE REALISTIC:

I will study in the library for two hours three days this week.

How about your anticipated hurdle? Did it actually emerge? If so, were you able to overcome it effectively? Did you discover other impediments? Furthermore, was your time frame appropriate for completing the Personal Action Statement?

Finally, examine your reward. Did you identify a reward that is meaningful to you? Your reward should urge you to finish a task and make you feel good about succeeding. Dangle a reward in front of yourself that you really want—and can have!

Answering these and similar questions will help you analyze what learning strategies do and do not work for you. It takes practice to develop effective Personal Action Statements, but the practice is worthwhile. Not only will you be learning about valuable college study strategies, but you will also be learning about *yourself!*

Conclusion: Creating Academic Success

Your success in college depends on a combination of factors: your behaviors in and out of class, your attitude and commitment to working hard, your awareness of key learning strategies, and your commitment to apply and assess these strategies in your daily life. The following checklist contains elements that directly relate to success, satisfaction and, ultimately, graduation from college. As the year progresses, periodically review the checklist with the goal of accomplishing as much as you can in order to keep yourself on the track to academic success.

KEYS TO A SUCCESSFUL ACADEMIC YEAR

1. **Be aware of *why* you are attending college as well as *what* you expect to get out of college.** Whose decision was it to attend college—yours or your parents? Are you attending the college of your choice? Do you

intend to graduate from this or from another college? What do you expect to accomplish in college? Be honest with yourself and clear in your goals.

2. **Know what is *expected of you* in each subject.** Read each syllabus. Make an appointment with each instructor. Attend all classes. Go to review sessions or form your own study group. *Ask . . .* and then write down the answers!

3. **Manage your time *wisely*.** Establish a routine; be aware of the dangers of too much free and unstructured time. Muster the self-discipline to say "no" to tempting people and activities. Also, create a balance among your academic, personal, and social/leisure lives. Periodically assess your priorities: Do you typically place your academic responsibilities *before* your social aspirations? Do you allow yourself fun time between the academic and personal demands on your time?

4. **Develop and *use* effective methods of study.** Create a study system that works for you; choose, use, and evaluate recommended learning strategies. Form good study habits *early* in the year.

5. ***Involve yourself* in college life.** Students who participate in academic, social, and personal campus activities tend to do better academically. Create a link between yourself and other people within the college community. Make a commitment to:
   - Join a student organization or club related to your interests or major.
   - Obtain a campus job.
   - Participate in academic support services, such as tutoring, group study sessions, and workshops, or become a tutor or peer educator.
   - Go to campus cultural events, such as guest speakers, fine arts productions, and museum exhibits.
   - Participate in intramural sports and other extracurricular activities.

6. ***Avoid* these hazards:**
   - Mishandling of your personal freedom and time.
   - Misuse of alcohol and drugs.
   - Mishandling of your personal health.
   - Mishandling of *your best interests*.

pause... *and reflect*

Refer to the previous list, "Keys to a Successful Academic Year." As a starting point in your college career, where would you place yourself?

For *each* of the six items, write a short paragraph assessing yourself at this point. Include *what you have done* as well as *what you still need to accomplish*.

try it out!

Use Figure 1.1 to try out a Personal Action Statement by choosing one of the items that you still "need to accomplish" for a successful academic year. Use the following example as a model for your own Personal Action Statement.

EXAMPLE OF A PERSONAL ACTION STATEMENT

1. I will: *become more involved in campus life by obtaining an on-campus job.*
2. My greatest hurdle to achieving this is: *not knowing where campus jobs are advertised.*
3. I will eliminate this hurdle by: *(1) asking my advisor about job listings during our meeting on Wednesday, and (2) inquiring at the Career Services Office.*
4. My time frame for completing this is: *by Thursday of this week.*
5. My reward for achieving this is: *the self-satisfaction of knowing that I began looking for a job EARLY in the semester!*

Your personal action statement.   FIGURE **1.1**

1. I will: _____

_____

_____

2. My greatest hurdle to achieving this is: _____

_____

_____

3. I will eliminate this hurdle by: _____

_____

_____

4. My time frame for achieving this is: _____

_____

5. My reward for achieving this is: _____

_____

_____

CHAPTER 1	CHAPTER 2	CHAPTER 3	CHAPTER 4	CHAPTER 5	CHAPTER 6	CHAPTER 7	CHAPTER 8
Academic Success	Managing Time	Study Environment	Active Listening	Reading Textbooks	Enhancing Memory	Test Success	Continuing Success

CHAPTER 2

Managing Your Time

FOCUS QUESTIONS

How effectively do I manage my time each day?

Why do college students often have difficulties managing their time productively?

What are five essential strategies for successful time management?

CHAPTER TERMS

After reading this chapter, define (in your own words) and provide an example for each of the following terms:

- academic planner
- procrastination
- self-regulating
- weekly block schedule

Controlling Your Time: Five Essential Ingredients

A challenge faced by many college students is how to effectively manage their daily usage of time. As a college student, you likely are—or soon will be—juggling a variety of responsibilities and tasks, both personal and academic. The freedom that you experience as an undergraduate college student often is unparalleled. For the first time, you are making many daily decisions without having a parent or teacher oversee you. For instance, you decide what time to awaken, whether to eat breakfast, whether to attend class or start an assignment, who to socialize with, and so on. Your decisions, and the subsequent consequences of these decisions, will determine whether or not you are successful in college. Read what one freshman wrote; his comments are typical of many first-time college students.

"Time management is my biggest problem. When I have to choose between leisure time and study time, leisure time always wins. I end up cramming the night before a test. One of my roommates, on the other hand, starts studying a week ahead of time for his exams and does much better than I. My problem is that nobody is here to make me study. In high school, my parents made me study; here at college, there always is something else I'd rather be doing." **—DEVON**

pause.... *and reflect*

Are you similar to Devon when making daily choices and decisions about academics and studying? Answer the following questions:

1. Do you have, or anticipate having, problems choosing study time over leisure time? Describe a situation when you *should have* studied but did not. Why didn't you study? What did you do instead? How could you have reacted differently? What might you do in order to choose study over leisure?

2. Do you need someone to "make you" study? If so, who can help you monitor your study time—a roommate, friend, tutor, or relative? What are some ways that you can develop the needed self-discipline and structure to focus on academics?

3. Some college students already possess **self-regulating** attitudes and behaviors and are able to consistently monitor their independent time. Self-regulating

students have developed the internal discipline, focus, and skills necessary to productively channel both time and energies. If you fall into this category, describe how you approach your study time. What strategies and attitudes do you adopt in order to focus on and complete projects, assignments, and other tasks?

4. Interview a present or former student whom you consider to be skillful about managing her time. What strategies does the student use? How did she develop those strategies? What suggestions can the student give you about having a productive yet balanced semester? Why would you describe this student as self-regulating?

Each of the following five ingredients is essential to the development of a successful system of study. As you read, consider how to incorporate each strategy into your day-to-day activities. The strategies are:

1. Use a weekly schedule
2. Use a planner
3. Use a calendar
4. Balance academic with social and personal demands
5. Avoid procrastination

Use a Weekly Schedule

At the start of each semester you will be faced with many new and unfamiliar situations—different classes and instructors, on-campus or off-campus jobs, and sometimes, even changes in your daily living arrangement. With these unfamiliar situations come unaccustomed expectations and responsibilities. Your most immediate need will be a schedule that provides an overview of what and where you should be for the week. The weekly schedule will help you structure your time as you develop sound habits and routines from the beginning of each semester.

Develop a weekly routine that includes:

○ 1. Class attendance and course work as your main priority.
○ 2. Regular slots for study throughout the week. Look for chunks of time during the day and evening when you are the freshest.
○ 3. Time *before* classes to refresh yourself about the day's topics.
○ 4. Time *after* classes to go over lecture notes, work on assignments, and complete readings.
○ 5. Ready access to a study location with minimal distractions.
○ 6. Time to take advantage of campus support services, such as the Tutorial Center, Writing Center, Counseling Center, and Career Services.

7. Time to attend extracurricular activities, such as fine arts productions, lectures and presentations, student organization meetings, and community service projects.

8. Time for personal commitments, such as a job, sports, or family responsibilities.

An added personal bonus that results from following these guidelines is that you are associating with others who are responsible, successful, and have similar values and interests. As a result, you will be creating a valuable social network for yourself.

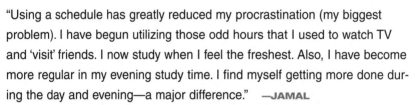

STUDENT VOICES

"I consider how difficult the class is for me and judge how much studying I will need. Studying earlier in the day helps me concentrate better because I am not tired. Also, I reduce my study time because I am reviewing after class when my recall is the greatest. I concentrate better during short spurts; therefore, I take advantage of the time between classes and small periods throughout the day." —RICARDO

"Using a schedule has greatly reduced my procrastination (my biggest problem). I have begun utilizing those odd hours that I used to watch TV and 'visit' friends. I now study when I feel the freshest. Also, I have become more regular in my evening study time. I find myself getting more done during the day and evening—a major difference." —JAMAL

The **weekly block schedule** (Figure 2.1) provides a visual representation of your week. By filling in the blocks you build a "picture" of your typical week. *Follow these STEPS when creating a weekly schedule:*

1. *First*, write in activities that you *must* do at *fixed* times, such as classes and labs, employment, commuting times, established meetings or appointments, certain family responsibilities, and practice for athletics, band, and so forth. Can you think of other established activities for *your* typical week?
2. *Next*, fill in those events for which you can establish your own times to work on and complete. Include three types of activities: *academic* (homework, study, tutoring), *personal* (meals, sleep, household tasks, errands), and *social and leisure* (calls/e-mails, exercise, "down time").

Two students' weekly block schedules are displayed in Figure 2.2. Note the differences between the two. Although each student approached the schedule with differing amounts of information and detail, both evaluated their schedules as being effective for them.

Block format for a weekly schedule.   FIGURE **2.1**

MONDAY	TUESDAY	WEDNESDAY	THURSDAY	FRIDAY	SATURDAY	SUNDAY
7:00	7:00	7:00	7:00	7:00	7:00	7:00
8:00	8:00	8:00	8:00	8:00	8:00	8:00
9:00	9:00	9:00	9:00	9:00	9:00	9:00
10:00	10:00	10:00	10:00	10:00	10:00	10:00
11:00	11:00	11:00	11:00	11:00	11:00	11:00
noon	noon	noon	noon	noon	noon	noon
1:00	1:00	1:00	1:00	1:00	1:00	1:00
2:00	2:00	2:00	2:00	2:00	2:00	2:00
3:00	3:00	3:00	3:00	3:00	3:00	3:00
4:00	4:00	4:00	4:00	4:00	4:00	4:00
5:00	5:00	5:00	5:00	5:00	5:00	5:00
6:00	6:00	6:00	6:00	6:00	6:00	6:00
7:00	7:00	7:00	7:00	7:00	7:00	7:00
8:00	8:00	8:00	8:00	8:00	8:00	8:00
9:00	9:00	9:00	9:00	9:00	9:00	9:00
10:00	10:00	10:00	10:00	10:00	10:00	10:00
11:00	11:00	11:00	11:00	11:00	11:00	11:00
midnight	midnight	midnight	midnight	midnight	midnight	midnight

FIGURE **2.2** *Two examples of weekly block schedules.*

Student A

MONDAY	TUESDAY	WEDNESDAY	THURSDAY	FRIDAY	SATURDAY	SUNDAY
7:00	7:00	7:00	7:00	7:00	7:00	7:00
8:00	8:00	8:00	8:00	8:00	8:00	8:00
9:00 *class*	9:00	9:00 *class*	9:00	9:00 *class*	9:00	9:00
10:00 *class*	10:00 *class*	10:00 *class*	10:00 *class*	10:00 *class*	10:00	10:00
11:00 *class*	11:00	11:00 *class*	11:00 *class*	11:00	11:00	11:00
noon	noon	noon	noon	noon	noon	noon
1:00 *class*	1:00 *lab*	1:00 *class*	1:00 *lab*	1:00 *class*	1:00	1:00
2:00 *work*	2:00	2:00 *work*	2:00	2:00 *work*	2:00	2:00 *work*
3:00	3:00	3:00	3:00	3:00	3:00	3:00
4:00	4:00	4:00	4:00	4:00	4:00	4:00
5:00	5:00	5:00	5:00	5:00	5:00	5:00
6:00	6:00 S.I. for Biol.	6:00	6:00 S.I. for Biol.	6:00	6:00	6:00
7:00 *study*	7:00	7:00	7:00	7:00	7:00	7:00
8:00	8:00 *study*	8:00 *study*	8:00 *study*	8:00	8:00	8:00 *study*
9:00	9:00	9:00	9:00	9:00	9:00	9:00
10:00	10:00	10:00	10:00	10:00	10:00	10:00
11:00	11:00	11:00	11:00	11:00	11:00	11:00
midnight	midnight	midnight	midnight	midnight	midnight	midnight

Continued.

FIGURE **2.2**

Student B

MONDAY	TUESDAY	WEDNESDAY	THURSDAY	FRIDAY	SATURDAY	SUNDAY
7:00	7:00	7:00	7:00	7:00	7:00	7:00
8:00	8:00 *breakfast*	8:00	8:00 *breakfast*	8:00	8:00	8:00
9:00 *breakfast*	9:00 *Chem review*	9:00 *breakfast*	9:00 *Chem review*	9:00 *breakfast*	9:00	9:00
10:00 *English class*	10:00 *Chemistry*	10:00 *English class*	10:00 *Chemistry*	10:00 *English class*	10:00 *workout*	10:00
11:00	11:00 *lunch*	11:00 *laundry*	11:00	11:00	11:00 *get ready*	11:00 *church*
noon *lunch*	noon *Chem lab*	noon *lunch*	noon *lunch*	noon *lunch*	noon *begin job*	noon *brunch*
1:00 *History class*	1:00	1:00 *History class*	1:00 *Writing Center*	1:00 *History class*	1:00	1:00
2:00 *Theater class*	2:00	2:00 *Theater class*	2:00	2:00 *Theater class*	2:00	2:00 *pack*
3:00 *review notes*	3:00 *Health class*	3:00 *review notes*	3:00 *Health class*	3:00 *pack*	3:00	3:00 *drive school*
4:00	4:00	4:00 *Big Bro./Sis.*	4:00	4:00 *travel home*	4:00	4:00
5:00 *workout*	5:00 *dinner*	5:00 *workout*	5:00 *dinner*	5:00	5:00 *dinner*	5:00 *dinner*
6:00 *dinner*	6:00	6:00 *dinner*	6:00	6:00 *dinner*	6:00 *get ready*	6:00
7:00 *study group*	7:00 *review notes*	7:00 *Chem tutoring*	7:00 *read History*	7:00	7:00 *to go out*	7:00 *English ?*
8:00 *for Chem*	8:00 *Economics club*	8:00 *break*	8:00 *TV break*	8:00 *get ready*	8:00	8:00 *History ?*
9:00 *TV break*	9:00	9:00 *study Health*	9:00 *study Theater*	9:00 *to go out*	9:00	9:00 *Theater*
10:00 *study Health*	10:00 *prep for class*	10:00 *floor meeting*	10:00 *finish English*	10:00	10:00	10:00 *homework*
11:00 *sleep*	11:00 *sleep*	11:00 *sleep*	11:00 *sleep*	11:00	11:00	11:00 *sleep*
midnight	midnight	midnight	midnight	midnight *sleep*	midnight *sleep*	midnight

FOR STUDENT B:

- The *darkened blocks* represent weekly activities established at fixed times.
- The *outlined blocks* represent times devoted to academic activities outside of class, including reviewing class notes, studying, and tutoring. Student B actually color-coded these outlined blocks according to subject.

pause.... *and reflect*

Some students (such as Student B) are more productive when they fill in nearly all of the blocks in their weekly schedule. They favor the structure of prearranged specific daily activities, including meals, sleep, study for each subject, and even breaks. Others (such as Student A) find this technique too restrictive and prefer to fill in only those blocks representing the most important activities.

- How about you? Are you more similar to Student A or Student B?
- Are you more productive when you plan details ahead of time or when you leave blocks open for spontaneous decisions and changes?
- What type of schedule are you more likely to follow?
- What type of activities should you be writing down in your weekly block schedule?

STUDENT VOICES

"By making a weekly schedule, I realized how many demands there are on my time. The schedule helps me complete my work and still have time for family and leisure. Last semester I was *always* rushing to get things done. This semester I am making better judgments about my time, which is reducing the stress in my life. I could not survive without a schedule and would recommend a schedule to *every student,* especially those students juggling many responsibilities." **—NORA**

"A weekly schedule helps me see what is due for the week and figure out what needs to be studied each day. Also, each night I make a schedule of classes, work, errands, and homework that I need to do the following day. And, I get such a feeling of accomplishment crossing off the things that I've finished!" **—BRAD**

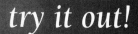

try it out!

1. Develop a weekly block schedule for yourself for the current semester (use Figure 2.1). Refer to the two steps described previously:
   - Fill in activities with *fixed* times.
   - Then fill in activities with *flexible* times.
2. Refer to the guidelines on pages 17–18. Consider each of the eight items when setting up your schedule.
3. After filling in your weekly block schedule, *use* it. Place it in a location for ready referral, such as over your desk, beside your calendar, near your computer screen, or in your book bag or planner. This weekly schedule will provide you with a framework for establishing your day-to-day routine; thus refer to it often, especially at the start of each semester.
4. After several weeks, **Assess Your Success** by answering these questions:
   - Overall, did the schedule provide you with a needed framework for establishing your daily routine?
   - Should you have more or fewer activities and details in your schedule?
   - Should you use another format, different design, or color coding for your schedule?
   - Did you refer to your schedule regularly? Why or why not?
   - Will you continue to use a weekly schedule? Why or why not?

Use a Planner

An **academic planner** is a day-to-day log, either in book or electronic format, reminding you of tasks to be accomplished. It is crucial to successfully planning and juggling schoolwork with personal and social activities. A well-used planner is invaluable for keeping you on track with your many and varied plans and responsibilities. Acquire a planner that easily fits in your book bag, backpack, or purse. Carry it with you and *use it daily* to write down reminders.

FOR THE DAY

Jot down and prioritize what you plan to do, including:

○ *Academic* responsibilities for each course.

○ *Personal* commitments or tasks, such as shopping, visiting a relative, or going to the bank.

○ *Social* plans, such as a call home or a date with friends.

FOR THE WEEK

○ Examine each course syllabus for *upcoming* lecture topics, readings, assignments, and test dates.

○ Note *extracurricular* activities, such as meetings, athletic obligations, and noncredit classes.

○ Be aware of *special commitments*, such as a doctor's appointment, a meeting with your advisor, a tutorial appointment, a theatrical production, or a birthday celebration.

FOR THE SEMESTER

Identify key academic dates, including:

○ Deadline for adding or dropping courses.

○ Deadline for course withdrawal.

○ Midterm period.

○ Final exam days and times.

○ Due dates for long-term course projects or papers.

○ Course registration for next term.

○ Breaks.

Use a Calendar

 calendar provides a long-term overview of your academic year. Use a calendar for a broad view of each semester. When you fill in important semester dates on a calendar, you create a visual picture of upcoming months, although with considerably less detail than your weekly block schedule.

Use a calendar in a similar, though less specific, manner as a planner: chart key *academic* dates and assignments, projects, and papers, as well as special *social* occasions (such as someone's birthday or a friend's wedding) and *personal* events (such as the deadline for filing taxes or a vacation). Place the calendar in a visible location for daily reference—near your computer, over your desk, or on the kitchen bulletin board. Publishers often place calendars within academic planners; note whether your planner provides monthly calendars that are large enough for you to write in and use.

A student's calendar for November is reproduced in Figure 2.3.

A student's calendar for November.

FIGURE   2.3

SUNDAY	MONDAY	TUESDAY	WEDNESDAY	THURSDAY	FRIDAY	SATURDAY
register for spring term this week	1	2	3	4	5	6 Melissa is visiting
7 Melissa	8 Math test Chap. 7-9	9	10	11	12 Spring work application due	13 march in Vets' Day parade
14	15	16	17	18 Intr. Religion term paper due	19 Accounting test #3	20 Begin break!
21	22	23 Dentist appt.	24	25 Thanksgiving	26	27
28 travel to school	29 classes resume	30 Geography group presentation				

try it out!

If you don't already have a *planner* and a *calendar*, buy them now!

1. Fill in the planner by referring to the lists (in the previous section) of what to write down "for the day," "for the week," and "for the semester." Check off each item as you mark the information in your planner. Continue using the planner, carrying it with you throughout the day.

2. Fill in the calendar with those major events that you want to track throughout the year. Place it in a location for easy reference.

3. **Assess Your Success:** Did you use your planner daily—that is, did you write in activities and reminders and refer to it consistently? How about your calendar? Did it help you to write down major events and due dates? What is the most useful aspect of your time management system thus far? What changes will you make in order to build a more effective and efficient time management system for you?

"Time management is a critical priority for studying, but I didn't realize it until this year. Previously, I lacked the self-discipline to follow a schedule and didn't think it would be useful. *Now* I realize how much it can help! I bought a huge desk calendar to write in all my major assignments, tests, quizzes, and readings that are due throughout the term. Not only do I now have more free time, but I actually have a better attitude toward studying!" —JENNIE

Balance Academic with Social and Personal Demands

College students often experience a conflict between their academic requirements and their social desires. It is in students' best *academic* interest to go to sleep before midnight. However, *social* activities often do not happen until late at night or even in the early morning hours. In both dormitories and off-campus complexes, late-night social activities are abundant and appealing. Friends will call or stop by to chat, watch TV, play music or video games, accompany you to a party, or ask you to go to an off-campus restaurant or bar. These late-night social activities are tempting and alluring to the college student who wants relief from academic demands as well as the chance to build a social network and personal sense of belonging.

However, over time, late-night socializing results in students who:

- Become severely sleep-deprived.
- Miss classes.
- Are in a dazed, passive mode when they do attend classes.
- Do not put in quality study time during the day (instead, they are sleeping!).
- Have problems organizing, understanding, and remembering subject matter.

. . . all of which contribute to *lower academic performances.* So beware: late-night socializing and partying can become a potent and dangerous habit!

On the other hand, some students, especially those of nontraditional ages, have personal demands that can supersede their academic demands. Time tending to family responsibilities, particularly children, and employment hours can easily push aside academic requirements.

Following are some strategies to help create a balance between your academic and your social/personal desires and demands:

1. *Prioritize.* Make a daily list of tasks according to their order of importance.

2. *Write down what to accomplish and when to accomplish it*, and then display your list for family and friends to see.

3. *Make others*—friends, family, and employers—*aware of your needs* and *time constraints*, and ask for their *cooperation*.

4. Don't let feelings of guilt guide you in an unproductive direction. Instead, *transform feelings of guilt* into *productive* and *useful behaviors* related to attaining success in your coursework.

5. *Don't overcommit yourself.* "Down time" is a necessity, not a luxury.

6. *Combine academic and social activities.* Find, or create, an environment that provides you with both solid academic activity and enjoyable social connections. Examples are study groups, tutorial or writing center services, campus organizations (such as a biology club or commuter student organization), or other groups that require study hours (such as a fraternity, sorority, or athletic team). For example, Devon (see the following "Student Voices") partially solved his time management problems by such a tactic.

"A help to me this semester, believe it or not, is pledging a fraternity. We have study sessions every Monday through Thursday from 6:00–8:00 P.M. in the library. This helps me, especially since the sessions are mandatory. If I don't go, I get into trouble. I have to hand in all my test grades to the scholastic chairman; if I don't get a 2.0, they won't let me in. This makes me want to do my best and is an added incentive." **—DEVON**

STUDENT VOICES

pause.... *and reflect*

1. Do you have problems balancing academic demands with personal responsibilities and/or social events?

2. When faced with a choice between attending to class work or taking care of personal obligations or social desires, what do you usually do?

3. Is it difficult for you to say "no" to other people's requests, demands, or temptations?

4. Follow these steps:
   - Identify your primary *academic* obligations for this week.
   - Next, identify your current *personal* responsibilities.
   - Identify your current *social* desires and events.

- Choose *one* of the six strategies described previously. Explain how you will use this strategy to assist you with managing the activities you listed above.

Avoid Procrastination

We all are guilty of **procrastination** at various times in our daily lives, be it paying a bill, looking for a summer job, writing a thank-you note, or doing the laundry. Still, constantly putting off responsibilities and tasks can be a major problem for college students, particularly for the important academic tasks of studying for exams, writing term papers, and keeping up with weekly reading assignments.

Procrastination causes undue stress, not to mention poor performance. Underlying causes of procrastination are often complex and varied. However, having an awareness of *why* you are delaying a task often helps you tackle and complete it. The following list describes some of the common reasons people procrastinate.

REASONS FOR PROCRASTINATION

- **Being a perfectionist.** You want to be uncompromisingly "perfect" at this activity and don't want to do the activity unless you are able to achieve your unrealistically high expectations. Since perfection is essentially impossible to achieve, you continue to postpone the activity.
- **Avoiding failure.** You are concerned that you will fail or perform inadequately and, as a result, will disappoint yourself and others. Therefore, you procrastinate in order to steer clear of a poor grade—and subsequent failure.
- **Avoiding success.** You are concerned that, as a result of your achievements, you will be expected to handle additional, more difficult, and/or burdensome responsibilities—responsibilities that you simply don't want!
- **Being rebellious.** You disagree with *why* you should do an activity, dislike *who* you associate with the activity (such as an assignment from a professor you dislike), or dislike the *task itself* (such as reading from a text) and, therefore, put off the activity out of resentfulness or defiance.
- **Feeling overwhelmed.** You consider the task or assignment to be of overbearing proportions and do not know *where* or *how* to begin. Or, you feel overburdened by multiple tasks and decisions and can't seem to get a handle on how to start tackling these activities.
- **Managing time poorly.** You don't plan ahead, use written schedules, or prioritize. You allow less significant tasks or events to get in the way.
- **Being lazy.** You want to avoid the effort and work involved in completing the task.

pause.... *and reflect*

Identify one task, assignment, activity, or decision that you *should* complete within the next week but that you have been putting off.

WHY are you putting off doing this? Use the list of reasons to describe the basis for your procrastination.

STRATEGIES TO OVERCOME PROCRASTINATION

1. **Know what you should accomplish.** You are more likely to complete a task that you clearly understand. Therefore, know the expectations and what you are to undertake. If you are uncertain about what you should accomplish, *ask!*

2. **Determine deadlines.** Have a preset time limit for completing the whole task and, if appropriate, various steps of the task. People tend to follow deadlines established by *other people* (as opposed to self-imposed deadlines). Therefore, if your instructor does not provide a strict deadline, ask another person—a classmate, roommate, or peer tutor—to establish a reasonable, written deadline for you.

3. **Use schedules/planners/calendars.** Write down *what* you want to do and *when* you will do it. You are more likely to accomplish a task that you write down on paper.

4. **Prioritize.** Assign a level of importance to all tasks. Then categorize activities according to:
   - Will work on today.
   - Will work on today if time.
   - Will save for another day.

5. **Break a task into a series of steps.** Large tasks seem less overwhelming and more approachable if you view them as a series of steps, as opposed to a gigantic whole. At the very least, identify one step that you can do; then do it!

6. **Do the unpleasant task first.** Get the distasteful activity out of the way early and then work on easier or more desirable activities.

7. **Change how you think about the task.** Instead of thinking of the activity as "dreaded" or "terrible," consider it as a practical *means to an end*, such as, a course that completes a curriculum requirement, a grade in order to pass a course, or a term paper that gives you research and writing experience.

8. **Have fun with the activity.** See if you can be imaginative with the task, such as adding color and other creative elements to a written assign-

ment. Or, you can invent a game or competition for yourself, such as beating a previous time for completing the task or keeping pace with a classmate's score. Sharing and collaborating with other task-minded students can be an enjoyable method for dealing with difficult or disliked subjects.

9. **Establish rewards as personal incentives for completion.**

   - *Extrinsic rewards:* Compensate yourself by watching a favorite TV program, going out with friends, or buying a new CD.
   - *Intrinsic rewards:* Recognize the personal sense of satisfaction that you receive when you've completed the task. Relish the sense of accomplishment you feel when you are done and can "check off" the item!

STUDENT VOICES

"Time management is my absolute worst skill. I tend to procrastinate quite a bit. I get my work done, but I always just squeak in under the deadline. This year, however, I've been forcing myself to work when I *should,* rather than when I feel like it." —CHARISE

"Making written schedules actually helps me organize my day and seize wasted time. For example, instead of reading a magazine while waiting at the hairdresser's for my appointment, I read an assignment. When I feel organized, my stress level drops tremendously. I feel on top of my assignments instead of overwhelmed by them." —JESS

try it out!

Refer back to the task, assignment, or decision that you have been putting off (page 29) and the "Strategies to Overcome Procrastination" (page 29). Identify a strategy that you will use in order to accomplish the task *this week.* Write a short paragraph explaining the strategy. Be specific about *what* and *how* you will complete the task.

In one week's time, **Assess Your Success:** Did you complete the task? Did the strategy help you to complete it? What other strategies will you use to focus your attention and energies on completing an "unpleasant" activity?

Personal Action Statement:
Applying Time Management Techniques

As described in Chapter 1, a Personal Action Statement is a step-by-step, written plan of a specific strategy—in this case, a time management strategy—that you are committing yourself to do. Before developing your own Personal Action Statement, examine the three examples provided below and answer these questions:

1. What are the differences among the plans?
2. Which students created plans that likely will result in successful outcomes? Why?

STUDENT A

1. I will study more for chemistry.
2. My greatest hurdle to achieving this is socializing.
3. I will eliminate this hurdle by socializing less.
4. My time frame for achieving this is soon—before the next test.
5. My reward for achieving this is "A's" in the class.

STUDENT B

1. I will study psychology for an hour after lunch each weekday.
2. My greatest hurdle to achieving this is afternoon soap operas on TV.
3. I will eliminate this hurdle by not watching *All My Children* Monday, Wednesday, and Friday and not watching *One Life to Live* Tuesday and Thursday. This will leave me with an added hour each afternoon.
4. My time frame for achieving this is to begin on Monday.
5. My reward for achieving this is that I can start catching up with my reading assignments and thus feel better about the class and myself.

STUDENT C

1. I will use a calendar to write down due dates for all courses.
2. My greatest hurdle to achieving this is the lack of exact due dates in two of my subjects.
3. I will eliminate this hurdle by penciling in estimates of due dates in my planner.
4. My time frame for achieving this is to fill in dates this weekend.
5. My reward for achieving this is a better sense of organization in my daily life.

try it out!

Learning Style and Time Management

Being able to effectively manage your time is a crucial element of a successful system of study. By linking *how* you learn best (your learning style or preference) with *ways* to learn (strategies), you will be better able to refine time management methods that are effective for you.

1. Write your four-letter "type" (as identified in Chapter 1):

   E   Extraversion   or   **I**   Introversion,

   S   Sensing   or   **N**   Intuition,

   T   Thinking   or   **F**   Feeling, and

   J   Judging   or   **P**   Perceiving.

2. Using Figure 2.4, find the headings representing your preferences (Extraversion or Introversion, Sensing or Intuition, and Judging or Perceiving) and refer to the left-hand column labeled "Learning Preferences." Do the learning preferences generally describe you when you are studying and learning?

3. Refer to the corresponding column "Time Management Strategies." Place a check (✓) in the circles next to the strategies that you *do* use *regularly*.

4. Additionally, if you know whether you prefer learning via *visual, auditory,* or *tactile/kinesthetic* means, take note of those time management strategies that are labeled accordingly: Visual = [V], Auditory = [A], Tactile/ Kinesthetic = [T/K].

Time management strategies and learning preferences.   FIGURE **2.4**

LEARNING PREFERENCES*	TIME MANAGEMENT STRATEGIES
Extraversion	
• Prefers variety and action. • Learns by talking, discussing, and clarifying ideas aloud. • Prefers to see how others do assignments.	○ Plan small blocks of study time with periodic, limited social breaks. ○ Find a committed, task-oriented study partner or study group. [A] ○ Participate in instructor-led or peer-led review sessions, or seek a tutor to regularly review notes and talk through assignments. [A]
vs. Introversion	
• Prefers time to think and reflect. • Prefers checking work with a familiar, trusted person. • Prefers to listen to others discuss topics.	○ Schedule large blocks of study time. ○ Establish a relationship with a peer tutor or a classmate who is doing well in the course. Regularly check your work with that person. [A] ○ Regularly attend small-group tutorial/review sessions in order to establish an ongoing relationship with others. [A]
Sensing	
• Is patient with details. • Prefers concrete, sequential activities.	○ Develop a routine from the start of each term. ○ Set up a detailed, structured, written schedule for the week that corresponds to daily needs and activities. [V] ○ Determine and then write down an appropriate amount of time to complete assignments for each subject. [V]
• Is impatient when details become complicated.	○ Study complicated subjects when you feel fresh. ○ Schedule tutorial help or instructor guidance for complex subjects. [A] ○ Allow extra time for lab work and application activities, especially for difficult subjects. [T/K]
vs. Intuition	
• Prefers to use imagination to come up with possibilities. • Likes solving new problems.	○ Create a schedule that *varies your activities.* Use contrasting colors and designs to differentiate activities. [V] ○ Be *flexible;* allow for big blocks of time to work on new assignments; anticipate slowdowns as you progress.
• Dislikes repetitive routine.	○ *Create an interest* for routine, detailed assignments, such as determining a *personal purpose* for accomplishing the task. Or, set personal *goals and rewards,* using a fanciful chart to keep track of your progress. [V] ○ Focus on broader meanings and connections among assignment topics. ○ Do the routine in differing places, or move about as you accomplish the task. [T/K] ○ Vary *how* you approach routines, such as scheduling time to work with others for routine matters. [A] *(continued)*

FIGURE **2.4** *Continued.*

| LEARNING PREFERENCES* | TIME MANAGEMENT STRATEGIES |

Judging

- Prefers to make a plan and have things settled and decided ahead of time.
- Likes to have clear structure.
- Prefers to finish one project before starting another.
- Usually has mind made up; may decide things too quickly.
- Lives by standards and schedules not easily changed.

○ Set up and use a detailed weekly block schedule. [V]
○ Decide and write down *when* and *where* you will study each subject. [V]
○ Talk to yourself as you write down daily appointments and tasks in your planner. [V] [T/K] [A]
○ Note due dates and plan accordingly—*break up* longer assignments into workable steps. [T/K]
○ Use color to signify dates and steps. [V]
○ Develop a *daily* priority list that includes academic assignments and personal responsibilities. [V] [T/K]

vs. Perceiving

- Prefers to stay flexible and avoid fixed plans.
- Prefers to make changes as problems arise.
- Likes what is new and different.
- Prefers to start many projects; may have difficulty finishing all of them.
- Deals well with unplanned, unexpected activities, often postponing the less pleasant activities.

○ Create a loose, less structured weekly schedule: note your fixed commitments; then allow for large blocks of time for spontaneous activities. [V]
○ Take advantage of your flexibility and adapt your schedule when unplanned things occur.
○ *Write down* starting and ending times for projects. [V] [T/K]
○ Space out tasks.
○ Note *due dates* on calendar, color-coding by subject. [V]
○ Be aware of your procrastination. Talk to yourself as you make a list of *when* you will work on an assignment. [V] [A]
○ Plan a reward for completion of unpleasant tasks, such as a physical activity. [T/K]
○ Write a due date *earlier* than needed. [V] [T/K]
○ Do unpleasant tasks *first.*

Key [V]   = Visual
         [A]   = Auditory
         [T/K] = Tactile/Kinesthetic

Source: Learning preferences material from *People Types and Tiger Stripes,* 3rd edition, by Gordon D. Lawrence. Center for Applications of Psychological Type, Gainesville, FL, 1993. Used with permission. This exercise is NOT a type indicator, nor does it replicate the Myers-Briggs Type Indicator® which is a validated instrument.

try it out!

Identify a strategy that you *do not* use on a consistent basis but which would likely help you to more effectively and efficiently manage your time for the upcoming week. Using Figure 2.5, write a Personal Action Statement for that strategy, using the guidelines outlined in Chapter 1:

○ Is your Personal Action Statement a commitment for action?

○ Have you identified specific steps that make your plan manageable?

○ Have you been realistic and honest with yourself? Did you identify a step or strategy that you intend to do, as well as anticipate hurdles and rewards for yourself?

○ Have you put both thought and time into your Personal Action Statement?

At week's end, **Assess Your Success.** Refer back to your Personal Action Statement and evaluate your performance by answering the following questions:

○ Did you accomplish what you set out to do?

○ Were you able to overcome any obstacles? Think about your experience and how successful you were with your reading.

○ If you were not satisfied, what additional behaviors or techniques can you implement in order to make your system of time management effective and efficient for you? Will you try these new strategies in the near future?

"I really was not planning on this Personal Action Statement helping me much; however, I have to admit that it worked well. This was the first time I ever made a real schedule for myself, and I've now grown accustomed to using it. With a set schedule, I see the day as a whole and actually get more done, especially in those hidden time areas throughout the day. It's odd to me that something this small can totally change my whole perspective on how, where, and when I spend my time." —CHRIS

STUDENT VOICES

FIGURE **2.5**   *Your personal action statement.*

1. I will: _____

_____

_____

2. My greatest hurdle to achieving this is: _____

_____

_____

3. I will eliminate this hurdle by: _____

_____

_____

4. My time frame for achieving this is: _____

_____

5. My reward for achieving this is: _____

_____

_____

Conclusion

Your decisions, and the subsequent consequences of these decisions, will determine how successful you are in college. Calendars, weekly schedules, and daily to-do lists are tools to assist you with the multitude of time management decisions. After all, *your* time is valuable; therefore, use it wisely!

1. Establish a weekly *routine* early each semester.
2. Use a *planner* every day; write down *what* and *when*.
3. Put important dates on a *calendar* so you will know what events are ahead and not be caught off guard.
4. Make wise decisions about *balancing* your academic responsibilities with social and personal activities.
5. Be aware of when you are *procrastinating*, and then use strategies that help you begin and complete the task.
6. Take charge; be *proactive*—don't allow others to control how *you* use *your* time.

CHAPTER 1	CHAPTER 2	CHAPTER 3	CHAPTER 4	CHAPTER 5	CHAPTER 6	CHAPTER 7	CHAPTER 8
Academic Success	Managing Time	Study Environment	Active Listening	Reading Textbooks	Enhancing Memory	Test Success	Continuing Success

CHAPTER 3

Controlling Your Study Environment

FOCUS QUESTIONS

What is the connection between *when* you study and *where* you study?

Describe an ideal study environment for yourself.

CHAPTER TERMS

After reading this chapter, define (in your own words) and provide an example for each of the following terms:

- external distractions
- internal distractions

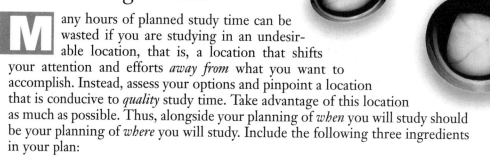

Controlling Your Study Environment: Three Essential Ingredients

Many hours of planned study time can be wasted if you are studying in an undesirable location, that is, a location that shifts your attention and efforts *away from* what you want to accomplish. Instead, assess your options and pinpoint a location that is conducive to *quality* study time. Take advantage of this location as much as possible. Thus, alongside your planning of *when* you will study should be your planning of *where* you will study. Include the following three ingredients in your plan:

1. Choose a suitable location.
2. Get organized.
3. Maximize concentration; minimize distractions.

Choose a Suitable Location

The following criteria will help you identify a desirable study location:

1. **Is this place *different from* where you sleep, eat, and socialize?** Although convenient, your dormitory room, apartment, or house often is full of distractions. Consider the multitude of distractions surrounding you in such a location—telephone, television, roommates, friends, family members, video games, a comfortable bed, personal chores, leisure activities, and so on. You are better off choosing a study place that you associate *only* with academics—such as a spare room, study lounge, empty classroom, tutorial center, or library carrel.

2. **Is this place away from direct foot traffic?** Choose a spot away from others. For example, a living room or a kitchen is often a high-traffic area, whereas other people rarely visit an extra room in your house. In the library, an upper-floor or corner table usually is better than the busy entrance way and main floor.

3. **Is this place readily accessible?** (Not accessible for other people who may distract you, but accessible for *you!*) You want a location that is available and easy to get to when you are ready for study. Consider locations nearby—for example, a study lounge in a residence hall or student union, an empty room in a classroom building, an on-campus or off-campus library, or a desk in the basement.

4. **Does this place provide you with the needed flexibility?** Consider your environmental preferences. For instance, if you study best when you are able

to spread out materials, choose a location with tables, such as at a library. Or, if you prefer to listen to soft music when studying, choose a spare room or a friend's apartment. If you like to eat or drink when studying, consider an empty meeting room in the student union. In addition, consider your present lifestyle. Do you need to fit study time around family obligations or an outside job? Personal issues—such as health needs, family demands, employment, home responsibilities, and other commitments—can affect not only *when* you are able to study but also *where* you are able to study.

"I've been studying more frequently in a library study room or a classroom building. I've found that library study rooms have fewer people and are quieter during the day. During the evening, I study in an empty classroom—it is quiet, spacious, and I can open and close windows and have more control. I've gotten significantly more work done."   **—CHAD**

STUDENT VOICES

try it out!

Rating Your Study Environment

Location A: What specific location do you use most often for study?

_____

Location B: What other location do you also use?

_____

Rate locations A and B by answering the four questions below. Use the following point scale:

"Yes"	=	2 points
"Somewhat"	=	1 point
"No"	=	0 points

Locations
A   B

1. Is this place different from where you sleep, eat, and socialize? ____ ____

2. Is this place away from direct foot traffic? ____ ____

3. Is this place readily accessible? ____ ____

4. Does this place provide you with the needed flexibility? ____ ____

Total Points ____ ____

Your Total Points for each location will be from a low of 0 to a high of 8. The higher your score, the more desirable the location is for study.

8 or 7 points: An *excellent* place to concentrate and study. Use it often.

6, 5, or 4 points: A *fair* study location. Make some changes to lessen distractions.

3, 2, 1, or 0 points: A *poor* study location. Work on reducing distractions or move to another location.

Write a short evaluation of your two locations. Consider these questions:

1. Which location had a higher score, A or B? Why?
2. What are your main distractions at each location?
3. Did your scores surprise you? Do you agree with the ratings?
4. What ways can you reduce distractions at each location?
5. What other locations would be worthwhile for study?

Get Organized

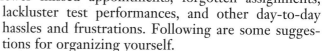

Organization is a vital component of effective, efficient study. When you organize your environment, you create an important sense of self-control and self-management. An active, "take-charge" approach toward arranging your surroundings often mirrors an active, "can-do" approach toward your course work. Also, as you organize yourself and your surroundings, you will be *preparing* to work. You will discover that, when organized, you encounter fewer missed appointments, forgotten assignments, lackluster test performances, and other day-to-day hassles and frustrations. Following are some suggestions for organizing yourself.

***Plan* ahead.** Keeping track of assignments, due dates, important events, and other short-term and long-term responsibilities is a fundamental aspect of personal planning. Use a written schedule—a planner, calendar, and daily to-do list—to prepare and plan in advance.

Have work *supplies* ready. Anticipate what you will need to complete assignments or activities. Keep your supplies in a central location, such as a desk or bookshelf. If you are a commuter student, keep your supplies in a portable container, such as a plastic storage box or tote bag. Store the container in your car or locker and carry what you need for classes, labs, or assignments.

SUPPLIES FOR COLLEGE STUDENTS

○ Textbooks

○ Supplemental CDs, study guides, lab guides, and so forth

○ Notebooks for each course—either three-ring binders or spiral bound

○ Labeled computer disks with carrying case

○ Pens, pencils, and highlighters

○ Access to a computer and printer

○ Paper—plain for printing, lined for notes

○ Index cards

○ Sticky notes

○ Dictionary and thesaurus

○ Stapler, paper clips, scissors, and hole puncher

○ Other: _____

Create *order* for yourself. An ordered environment will increase your overall work efficiency and productivity. A personal sense of neatness or orderliness differs from individual to individual. Know your preferences and tolerance in regard to cleanliness, room arrangement, and tidiness. Also, recognize that at times you'll be more productive if you rearrange or clean your study location *before* tackling your academic assignments.

try it out!

1. Review the list of college supplies above. Mark which ones you already have and which ones you still need to get. Are there other supplies that you should have for any of your classes this term? Where are you keeping the supplies so that you can easily locate and use them?

2. Do a thorough inspection of your study environment. Characterize the degree of neatness or cleanliness that is important to you and that results in your most productive work. Establish your environment accordingly; put supplies in proper receptacles, use shelves or drawers to store items, reduce clutter on your desk or tabletop, and create space to spread out work. If you have access to a camera, take a photo of the ordered setting; post the photo as a reminder of what your work area *should* look like!

Maximize Concentration; Minimize Distractions

Poor concentration results in inefficient use of your time. Distractions divert concentration and interrupt productive work. Therefore, the fewer the distractions, the better a location is for study. Distractions fall into two categories:

1. **External distractions** originate from a source *outside* of you. Examples are the TV, a computer, or noise.
2. **Internal distractions** originate from *within* you. Examples are your mind wandering or your lack of motivation.

"I commute to school and have explored suitable locations for study during blocks of time between classes. (The library is too quiet and too warm for me.) Sometimes I use the commuter lounge in the Student Union, especially in the mornings, when fewer people are there. However, when I really need to concentrate, I find an unused room in a classroom building. I'm able to spread out my materials, eat my lunch, and move about when necessary." —MELISSA

"I used to study in my dorm room because it was comfortable and convenient, but I found this was not suitable. I got distracted easily, whether it was a distant radio or someone talking in the hall. Plus, I had a tendency to take many breaks. I now study at the library at a remote desk that has no radios, no people talking, and nothing else to occupy my time. For a break, I bring candy along with me. When I feel bored, I move to another desk in the library." —JOSH

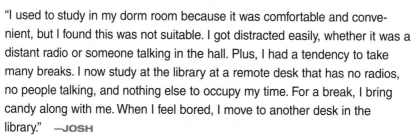

try it out!

Controlling Distractions

Beside each distraction listed in Figure 3.1, note:

1. Is the distraction *external* or *internal?*
2. How often are you bothered by this distraction: *often, sometimes,* or *rarely?*
3. What are ways to *reduce* or *eliminate* this distraction?

Rating common distractions.   FIGURE **3.1**

Distractions	E = external I = internal	O = often S = sometimes R = rarely	Ways to Reduce or Eliminate
○ Phone			
○ Television			
○ Boredom			
○ Computer (e-mail, instant message, games, etc.)			
○ Roommates or family members			
○ Noise or music			
○ Lack of interest			
○ Thinking about other activities or people			
○ People stopping by			
○ Laziness or lack of self-discipline			
○ Disorganization			
○ Worry			
○ Lack of goals for school or career			
○ Sleepiness			
○ Hunger			
○ Other responsibilities			
○ Not motivated			
Any others?			

pause... *and reflect*

1. Internal distractions tend to be more difficult to eliminate than do external distractions. Why?
2. Which type of distractions bothers you most—internal or external? Explain.
3. On the previous chart, put a "✓" in the circle next to your *top three* distractions. Consider several realistic, practical strategies for reducing each distraction. Ask for suggestions from others.

try it out!

Learning Style and Study Location

Identifying a study location compatible with your preferences and tolerances sometimes requires you to think unconventionally, that is, away from the usual, more popular choices of living spaces (dorm room, bedroom, or kitchen) or the campus library. You want to create a study environment that minimizes distractions while meeting your needs and preferences. The following steps will guide you when choosing a study location strategy compatible with your learning style.

1. Write your four-letter "type" (as identified in Chapter 1):

   E Extraversion   or   **I** Introversion,
   S Sensing   or   **N** Intuition,
   T Thinking   or   **F** Feeling, and
   J Judging   or   **P** Perceiving.

2. Using Figure 3.2, find the headings representing your preferences (Extraversion or Introversion and Judging or Perceiving) and refer to the left-hand column labeled "Learning Preferences." Do the learning preferences generally describe you when you are studying and learning?

3. Refer to the corresponding column "Study Location Strategies." Place a check (✓) in the circles next to the strategies that you *do* use regularly.

4. Additionally, if you know whether you prefer to learn using visual, auditory, or kinesthetic/tactile means, take note of those study location strategies that are labeled accordingly: Visual = [V], Auditory = [A], Tactile/Kinesthetic = [T/K].

Study location strategies and learning preferences.   FIGURE **3.2**

LEARNING PREFERENCES*   **STUDY LOCATION STRATEGIES**

Extraversion

- Likes to have people around.
  - ○ Choose a study location with *access to people,* such as a lounge, an empty classroom, or a computer lab.
  - ○ Go to a tutorial room or Homework Helper location in order to discuss your subject matter with others. [A]
- Easily distracted by people.
  - ○ Create a study environment that is *near* people and activities, so you don't feel isolated, but not in the middle of activities, since your concentration can be readily interrupted.

vs. Introversion

- Prefers uninterrupted quiet time.
- Prefers to work alone or with a few people.
  - ○ Choose a study location away from others—free of noise and distractions and where you can *talk aloud to yourself* [A] or *move about* [T/K] as you study.

Judging

- Prefers to make a plan and have things settled and decided ahead of time.
- Likes to have clear structure.
  - ○ Create a structured, traditional study environment for yourself. Have a desk, chair, lamp, and other supplies ready to use in an uncluttered, open study space. [V]

vs. Perceiving

- Prefers to stay flexible and avoid fixed plans.
- Prefers to make changes as problems arise.
- Likes what is new and different.
  - ○ Purposely move around and try new and different spaces for study. [T/K]
  - ○ Be creative with modifying your favorite study location—change posters, add pictures and colorful decorations, rearrange furniture, and make other novel modifications. [V] [T/K]

Key   [V]   = Visual
      [A]   = Auditory
      [T/K] = Tactile/Kinesthetic

Source: Learning preferences material from *People Types and Tiger Stripes,* 3rd edition, by Gordon D. Lawrence. Center for Applications of Psychological Type, Gainesville, FL, 1993. Used with permission. This exercise is NOT a type indicator, nor does it replicate the Myers-Briggs Type Indicator® which is a validated instrument.

try it out!

Identify a specific study location strategy that you will try *this week*. Using Figure 3.3, write a Personal Action Statement for the strategy, using the guidelines outlined in Chapter 1:

○ Is your Personal Action Statement a commitment for action?

○ Have you identified specific steps that make your plan manageable?

○ Have you been realistic and honest with yourself? Did you identify a step or strategy that you intend to do, as well as anticipated hurdles and rewards for yourself?

○ Have you put both thought and time into your Personal Action Statement?

As you use this location, be attentive to how effectively you work and concentrate. At the end of the week, **Assess Your Success.** Refer back to your Personal Action Statement and evaluate your success by answering these questions:

• Did you follow through with what you set out to do? Explain.

• Were you able to overcome hurdles? How prevalent were external and internal distractions?

• Did your reward provide a positive reinforcement for you?

• Are you satisfied with this location? Does it seem to fit your particular needs and lifestyle? What additional changes do you want to make? Is there a location that might be superior and that you will try?

Conclusion

Be mindful of *where* you study. Work at creating a suitable study environment—that is, a setting that maximizes productive use of your study time. Improve your concentration by minimizing both external and internal distractions. Finally, establish an ordered, uncluttered workspace for yourself.

Your personal action statement.

FIGURE **3.3**

1. I will: _____

   _____

   _____

2. My greatest hurdle to achieving this is: _____

   _____

   _____

3. I will eliminate this hurdle by: _____

   _____

   _____

4. My time frame for achieving this is: _____

   _____

5. My reward for achieving this is: _____

   _____

   _____

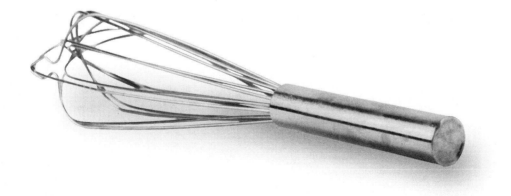

CHAPTER 4

Active Listening and Note Taking

FOCUS QUESTIONS

Why is active listening important?

How are active listening and selective listening similar and different?

CHAPTER TERMS

After reading the chapter, define (in your own words) and provide an example for each of the following terms:

- active listening
- listening cues
- nonverbal cues
- selective listening
- verbal cues

ESSENTIAL INGREDIENTS College Studying

Active Listening:
The Essential Ingredients

There is a difference between "listening to" and "hearing" information. You perceive sounds when you *hear* information. *Listening* implies more than just a physical act; *listening* is an *active* process—in addition to hearing information, you are *thinking* about the information. Good listening requires alertness and energy; you must pay attention and focus on *what* information is being presented, *why* you should know the information, and *how* you should represent the information in your notes. Therefore, **active listening** involves many decisions on the listener's part. When done well, note taking will help you to listen actively.

You will discover that, on a typical exam, the majority of information comes from material covered in class. Therefore, take notes! The purpose of class notes is twofold:

1. To help you *understand* class information.
2. To help you *remember* class information.

Active listening and note-taking skills are fundamental to college success. The following essential ingredients added *before*, *during*, and *after* each class will maximize your proficiency as a student:

1. Prepare before class.
2. Listen and take notes during class.
3. Follow up after class.

Prepare Before Class

The most essential strategy is to *go to class*. The importance of attending class cannot be overstated. Most of the information that will be on tests, as well as directions for assignments and papers, are covered in class. Copying someone else's notes is not the same as personally being in class to observe, listen to, and ask questions. Of course, illness and personal emergencies do arise. *If* you are unable to attend class, let the professor know via an e-mail or phone message. *Before the next class*, find out what was covered in class and any assignments you missed.

Prepare yourself physically for class; resting and eating well will improve your listening concentration. In addition, bring supplies, texts, and completed assignments. If your instructor places notes on a website or campus network drive, print out and take the notes with you to class. Try to arrive a few minutes early to get seated and ready to listen and take notes. You may find the following suggestions will assist you in preparing for class.

BRING AN APPROPRIATE TYPE OF NOTEBOOK

- A **loose-leaf paper and binder** provides you with the most *flexibility*. Use this type if you print copies of lecture information from a website, if you have handouts to insert within your notes, or if your instructor jumps from topic to topic during the lecture. Also, use loose-leaf paper if you prefer to spread out pages for an ordered overview of a topic or time period.
- A **spiral-bound notebook** tends to be the more *convenient* type of notebook since the paper is already packaged for you. If your instructor presents information in an orderly, straightforward manner, you might favor a spiral-bound notebook, especially one with pockets for handouts.

BRING WRITING UTENSILS

- **Ink pens** help you write *faster* and *clearer*. Also, your writing will last longer with ink pens rather than with lead pencils.
- **Lead pencils** generally will make your writing *slower* and *lighter*. However, use lead pencils if you do a lot of erasing, such as in a problem-solving mathematics or chemistry course.
- **Colored markers, pens, and pencils** can be used to provide *emphasis* for key words and phrases.

BE FAMILIAR WITH THE MATERIAL

- **Read, or at least skim through, text assignments or online information** to provide background and better understanding of ideas to be presented in the lecture. Consider keeping your text open during class for easy referral when (1) the instructor's lecture parallels the text information, (2) the instructor mentions the text frequently, or (3) the text presents the subject matter in a clear, easily understood format.
- **Look over your notes from the previous lecture** to refresh your memory about where that lecture ended and what topics were covered. This refresher provides a transition between class sessions and helps focus your attention on the current day's topic.
- **Look over written or online assignments** that the instructor likely will refer to during class.

pause.... *and reflect*

1. What should you do *before class* for each course you are enrolled in this term? Using Figure 4.1, fill in the chart indicating your preparation for each subject.

2. A universal recommendation is for students to choose a seat in the front of each classroom. When sitting in the front, you will be able to hear and see better. Name two other reasons why you should choose a seat in the front of a classroom.

FIGURE **4.1**   *Preparation by subject.*

Subject	Supplies needed for class	Type of preparation for class

"Two years ago, I had one exceptionally bad semester where I did nothing at all (this includes skipping most classes, some tests, and two finals). Afterward, I was on academic probation and then dismissed from college. I worked for two years. Now I'm trying college again with a different attitude. One thing that has influenced my performance is that I figured out what each class hour costs me. I added tuition, books, meals, housing, and all fees and divided the total by the number of class hours in a semester (256 for me). This semester, each class I miss costs me about $24.97!!! I figure since the class is paid for, I'll go and get my $25 worth!   —MICHAEL

Listen and Take Notes During Class

Creating notes is a major component of active listening and involvement during class. Note taking helps you to be more alert, to discriminate important points, and to organize information—all of which are keys to understanding and remembering. Take into account the following five factors as you listen and take notes during a class session.

1. LISTEN SELECTIVELY

Focus on *ideas*, not just words. Throughout the lecture, continually ask yourself, "What are the important points that the instructor is trying to get across?" Then write down enough information to help you understand those points. **Selective listening** involves an awareness of what *is* and *is not* important enough to write down. Thus, selective listening requires active decision making on your part. Instead of writing down everything the instructor says, choose main ideas and corresponding supporting points, including explanations and examples. As you listen, ask yourself the following questions, which will help you to pick out noteworthy ideas:

- "What is the *topic?*"
- "What do I need to *know* about the topic?"
- "Why is this topic *important?*"
- "What is an *example* of the topic?"
- "How did this event or procedure *come about?*"

If you are unsure of how much information to write down in your notes, it is best to err on the side of writing *too much*, rather than *too little*. When you review notes after class, you can highlight key points while eliminating redundant information.

During lectures, instructors give many clues as to what is and is not important. These clues are termed **listening cues.** Keep in mind: if your instructor thinks an idea is important, that idea likely will be on an upcoming test; thus, you want to capture the idea and related information in your notes.

Verbal cues are what your instructor *says* that signals an idea is important enough to write down. Examples of verbal cues are your instructor *repeats information* (making sure you hear and write it down), *pauses or slows down* when talking (giving you time to write down information), or *talks louder* (ensuring that you hear).

Nonverbal cues are what your instructor *does* that indicates an idea is important. Examples of nonverbal cues are your instructor *uses hand gestures* (to help explain important information), *points to words on the board* (to make sure you see and write the information), walks among students, *looking at students' notes* (to see if they are writing down correct information).

pause.... *and reflect*

What *verbal* and *nonverbal* cues do your instructors use to signal important ideas? Target a course in which you will be listening to lectures for the upcoming week. In class, be attentive to your instructor's cues. Keep a diary of your observations for the week.

Verbal cues:

_____

_____

Nonverbal cues:

_____

_____

2. TAKE CONCISE NOTES

In many classes, you will be quickly writing down numerous ideas; therefore, use as few words as you need to communicate these ideas. Here are some tips to help you be concise and succinct.

Write in phrases, not whole sentences. Focus on those words that convey *ideas* within statements. What words are necessary to write down in order to communicate these ideas? Usually, you can eliminate adjectives, adverbs, prepositions, and conjunctions and still get across the core meaning. Therefore, in your note taking, focus on the *subject* or *topic* and *what you need to know* about the topic, as illustrated below:

> *Instructor says:* "Both external and internal distractions contribute to inadequate attention spans of college students attending large, introductory-level lecture classes."

> *You write:* "external & internal distract's ⟶ poor attention of students in lecture classes"

> *After class:* You go over what you wrote and |BOX| the terms "external and internal distract's" for **emphasis** and add *examples* for **clarity:**

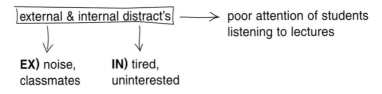

Use abbreviations and symbols. Accustom yourself to using abbreviations and symbols when taking notes. Both will help you reduce the quantity of writing necessary to get ideas across on paper. Repeat abbreviations and symbols within your notes so that they become familiar and identifiable to you. Here are some techniques for shortening words.

- Use beginning letters of words or phrases.

    "without" = w/o

    "overdose" = OD

    "sign on" = S.O.

    "as soon as possible" = asap

- Use beginning syllables.

    "anthropology" = anthro

    "demonstration" = demo

    "approximately" = approx

- Remove vowels, since the tendency is to recognize words by consonants.

    "explosion" = explsn

    "check" = chck

    "notebook" = notebk

- Use the beginning and end of words.

    "abbreviations" = abbrev's ; "continued" = cont'd ; "additional" = add'l

- Use common characters and symbols.

    ? = "I don't understand"

    @ = "at"

    $\longrightarrow$ = "linked to or causes"

    * or ! = "important"

- Use mathematical signs.

    > < represent "greater than/less than"

    = means "equal to"

    # for "number"

    ~ means "approximately"

    + for "and"

try it out!

Practice your note-taking skills: Imagine that you are listening to the following passage in a class. Create your class notes on a separate sheet of paper. Be *selective* (focus on important ideas), and be *concise* (write in phrases and use abbreviations and symbols).

Consider the difference between "hearing" and "listening." Hearing is simply the physical function of perceiving sound, whereas listening involves thoughtful attention to those sounds as received by an individual. There are three types of listening: casual, attentive, and evaluative. Casual listening is when one listens to understand but not necessarily remember. Examples include listening to a friend talk or to the radio or TV. Most of everyday listening is classified as casual listening. On the other hand, a high degree of remembering is a distinctive characteristic of attentive listening, which involves more thought, alertness, and energy than does casual listening. Most of college students' classroom listening should be of this type. Bear in mind that note taking helps an individual to listen attentively. The type of listening requiring the most thought process and energy is evaluative listening. For this category, not only does the listener want to remember, but he also intends to assess information heard. For instance, in a literature course, the instructor gives an assignment to attend a poetry reading and write a critique of a recited poem. The student would be listening to the poem with the intent of assessing critically—thus, evaluative listening. Taking written notes strengthens one's evaluative listening skills.

3. BE CLEAR

Make your notes understandable enough for *you*. After class, you should review the day's lesson; at this point, you will be able to further clarify ideas by rewriting information, adding explanations and examples, and integrating text material.

Thus, be generous with paper as you take class notes. Avoid cramming topics together on the pages. Instead, leave ample spaces between ideas, especially when you know that information is missing. Consider writing on one side of the paper only so that you will have the back to add information, if needed.

In addition, standardize a method for organizing your notes. Always place the subject, date, and topic at the start of the day's notes. As you write, consider the arrangement of ideas. Write main ideas at the left margin and then indent supporting ideas and details. Underline or capitalize headings. Use numbers or letters to itemize separate points. Where appropriate, categorize ideas and add formulas and other visual aids. Include examples from class, and allow space to add more examples and explanations later. Figure 4.2 exemplifies concise, clear, well-organized notes.

4. BE ACCURATE

To ensure that you are representing the ideas accurately within your notes, do the following.

Examine your notes *soon* after class. That is, go back over your notes while the information from the class is still fresh in your mind—usually within 24 hours after the class.

Sample class notes.   FIGURE **4.2**

Nutrition & Wellness — Oct. 9

"DIET & WEIGHT CONTROL" (cont'd)

Subject, date, and
topic at top of page.

Obesity is excessive enlargement of body's total
quantity of fat — 20% above ideal weight.

** Important ——→ know differ.**

Visual emphasis.

Overweight is measured for specific height, age,
& sex as 10% over ideal weight.

chart p. 115 text shows % of pop.

References to text.

Fat Cell Develop.:
1) Last trimester of pregnancy
2) First 1—2 yrs.
3) Adolescent growth period
   a) begin puberty
   b) end adult height/weight

Use of abbreviations
and symbols.

Topic in headings
with supporting
details numbered
beneath.

Ways to alter CELL size & #:
1) Modify early nutrition
   ex) gauge infant's formula intake
2) Exercise — early in body growth period depresses
   growth of new fat cells
                what if not early??

Spaces between
topics. Extra space
to add information
after class.

Weight Control (adults):
Weight fluctuates only slightly during yr. even though
annual food intake is 1600—1800 lbs.

Most establish equilibrium between energy input & output

energy in = energy out like a balancing seesaw!

Illustrations and
examples.

Consult your textbook, lab manual, or other reference source. If you notice a discrepancy between your class notes and the text or other written source, seek clarification from your instructor, a graduate assistant, or a peer educator.

Go over class information with peers. One of the most effective means for review of class notes is regular attendance at peer-lead study groups. If you are unable to locate formal study/review groups, establish your own by inviting classmates (who are serious, capable students) to join you weekly for collaborative review.

5. PAY ATTENTION

This is a key element of effective listening and note taking. Daydreaming is a problem for many students, but *physically* being in class is ineffective if you are not also *mentally* attending to class.

Consciously *want* to be alert. The foremost tactic for maintaining your concentration in class is willfully wanting to pay attention. Notice the following student's choice of the word *intend* when describing how she improved her alertness in her accounting course.

STUDENT VOICES

"I intended to pay closer attention in accounting class. I did have my moments of daydreaming, but, for the most part, I did listen and followed along with the material being presented. I actually knew how to do homework problems; it was a nice feeling!"   **—BERNICE**

Personal determination plays a huge role in attentiveness and concentration, even in boring or undesirable situations.

Participate in class. *Answer* questions. *Comment* on topics. *Ask* for clarification. Your involvement and participation can enliven a class lecture and keep you more alert.

Sit up front. Being able to see and hear better should help you to pay attention. Also, knowing you are highly visible to your instructor can motivate you to be more alert and involved in class.

Create physical movement. Bring a caffeinated drink (if permitted). Chewing on gum or candy can help keep your mind activated. Switch colored pens. Wiggle your leg; even slight movements can help you stay awake and focused.

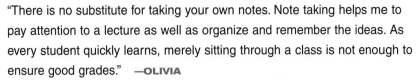

"There is no substitute for taking your own notes. Note taking helps me to pay attention to a lecture as well as organize and remember the ideas. As every student quickly learns, merely sitting through a class is not enough to ensure good grades." —OLIVIA

"Unlike in the past, I now look over my notes more frequently and actually read the text as assigned. Now I feel *much more* comfortable during class discussions since I am more familiar with the material, instead of hearing it for the first time right there in class." —JUSTIN

STUDENT VOICES

A NOTE ABOUT WEB NOTES

A growing number of instructors are posting lecture notes, often in the form of an outline or Microsoft PowerPoint presentation, on a website or on campus computers with a common network. Make hard copies of these notes and bring them to class, but also be prepared to take additional notes during class. For this type of course, consider in-class note taking as an opportunity to supplement and to clarify. Be alert to your instructor's emphasis of key points using verbal and nonverbal cues. As you listen, insert information and examples that help to explain ideas. Circle or highlight key terms and phrases. Use your system of abbreviations and symbols to illuminate important material. During class, you are beginning to create a study guide for yourself, as detailed in the following section. (After class, you still will need to review your notes and continue with your study guide; see Figures 4.3 and 4.4.)

Follow Up After Class

Review your class notes and create a study guide for yourself. To reduce the progression of forgetting, incorporate this step within 24 hours after a class. By immediately reviewing, you will be checking your understanding of class material. Do the following as you go over your notes.

- *Highlight* key words or phrases.
- *Condense* information.
- *Fill in* incomplete material.
- *Add* explanations and examples in your own words.
- *Refer* to text material.
- *Summarize* key points.
- *Think about* what you need to know for the upcoming quiz, exam, or discussion, and *develop questions* for yourself.

FIGURE **4.3** *Study guide with text references and summary.*

BIOLOGY   4/11
          class notes – Chap. 15, Carboxylic Acids

Carboxylic Acids contain the carboxyl grp.
       O   – a hydroxyl grp. Bonded to carbonyl C
       ‖
R – C – OH – Is polar, meaning it will form H+ bonds causing high
               melting/boiling pts.

Names: | see CHART in CHAP 15 |
1) Methanoic acid – ant & bee stings
2) Ethanoic acid – vinegar   ────→ | Will hydrogen bond cause
3) Propanoic acid – dairy products   high melt'g/boil'g pts? |
4) Butanoic acid – rancid butter
5) Oxalic acid – rhubarb
6) Citric acid – sour taste in lemon
7) Lactic acid – sour milk

Naming C.A.'s | full rules on p. 437 |
* oic ending
* the C on carboxylic acid is #1
* for anions, change to "-ate" ending & omit "acid"

DIMER – special H+ bonding structure CA's may take on.

| Note structure on p438 **GOOD TEST QUESTION** |

SUMMARY:
Carboxylic Acids contain the carboxyl group. They are long, straight changes
called fatty acids from hydrolysis of dietary fats. There are seven types,
named according to rules of oic, C on carboxylic acid & changing –ate to
acid. A dimer is a special H+ structure.

STUDY GUIDE created AFTER class
The following are after-class additions:

1. Numbers to organize listing

2. Additions from related text chapter

3. A written summary of key points   [notes contributed by Adrienne Runk]

Study guide for web-based notes.   FIGURE **4.4**

Web Notes	INTRODUCTION to GEOLOGY				Week Two
	CHARACTERISTICS OF SEDIMENTARY ROCKS				

Type of Rock	Sediment	Environment	Mineral	Chemical Composition	OTHER INFO
LIMESTONE	Calcite Shells (alike) ↓↑	Shallow warm oceans	Calcite (alike) ↓↑	CaCO3 (alike) ↓↑	1. carbonate sand & mud 2. has to be shallow & warm b/c organisms making the shells don't live in cold water 3. calcite dissolves in cold water
CHALK	Microscopic Calcite Shells	Quiet deep sea floor; organisms fall to the bottom when they die	Calcite	CaCO3	**SIMILAR to Limestone
CHERT	Tiny Silica Shells	↓↑ (alike) Quiet deep sea floor; colder water	Opal Quartz	SiO2	Siliceous Sediment ↓↑ (vs.)
EVAPORITES	Gypsum Halite	Dried lakes or oceans	Bypsum Halite Anhydrite	Gypsum-CaCO3 Halite-NaC1	1. Evaporite Sediment 2. made in desert climates—Death Valley, Persian Gulf
PEAT/COAL	Plant Debris	Swamp Bog	Coal Oil Gas	Carbon	1. pure organic matter 2. Function: preserves organic matter by keeping animals out that would eat it

Study Questions:
1. What are the 5 types of sedimentary rock?
2. Describe the composition, environment, and key features of each.
3. Which types are similar?

During class the student:
1. Added last column ("OTHER INFO") to write additional information.
2. Added phrases linking certain types: "↓↑ (alike)".
3. Highlighted the names of rocks and other terms.

After class the student:
4. Wrote three study questions on the back of the paper.

By adding, condensing, emphasizing, and organizing lecture information, you will be creating a valuable study guide for yourself. Figures 4.3 and 4.4 illustrate differing study guides. By reviewing and *doing something* with notes soon after class, you are immediately integrating study with note taking. That is, you are *learning* the subject matter while it is still fresh in your mind. This strategy is considerably more effective and efficient than the usual method of *only* reviewing class notes days—or even hours—before the exam. Since reviewing notes and creating a study guide *soon after class* is pivotal for understanding and remembering class information, incorporate this study strategy into your weekly routine from the beginning of the semester.

Review weekly. For an overview of the subject matter, each week skim through the study guides you have created from your class notes. This will help you see connections among topics. Reinforce these connections by saying key ideas out loud.

Use academic support services. *Regularly* participate in group study and review sessions. If you don't understand something, ask your instructor, a graduate student, or a peer tutor for an explanation.

Use the Cornell note-taking system. A popular method of note taking is the Cornell system, developed at Cornell University over 40 years ago (Pauk, 2001, pp. 236–41). A key component of this system is the wide, formal columns on each sheet of notepaper used for after-class study guides and review:

- A $2\frac{1}{2}$-inch "cue column" on the left side of the paper to develop questions, and
- A 2-inch strip at the bottom of the paper to write a summary.

The steps for the Cornell note-taking system are as follows:

1. *During* class, take notes using the six-inch space on the right side of the notepaper.
2. *Soon after class*, go back over your notes, filling in information.
3. Use the "cue column" to develop *questions* based on each key idea.
4. Cover the body of your notes (in the six-inch area) with a sheet of paper. *Recite the answer* to each question in the "cue column," checking your answer by uncovering the body of your notes. Repeat this step until your answers are correct.
5. Use the two-inch space at the bottom to write a concise *summary* of ideas on the page.
6. *Review* your notes right away to reinforce the material.
7. *Reflect* about the importance of the overall ideas.

Figure 4.5 illustrates the Cornell system of note taking.

Cornell system of note taking.   FIGURE **4.5**

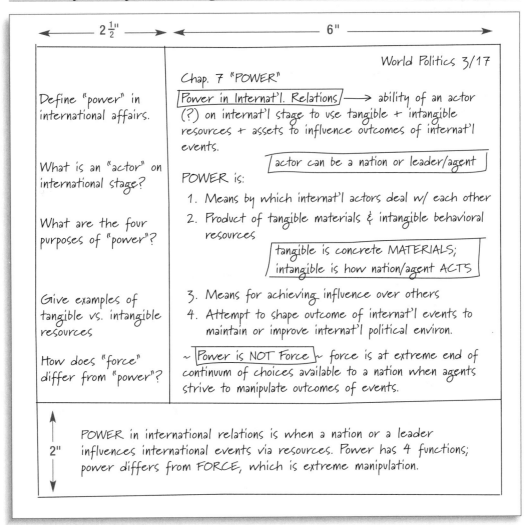

← 2 ½" →   ← 6" →

World Politics 3/17

Chap. 7 "POWER"

Define "power" in international affairs.

Power in Internat'l. Relations → ability of an actor (?) on internat'l stage to use tangible + intangible resources + assets to influence outcomes of internat'l events.

actor can be a nation or leader/agent

What is an "actor" on international stage?

POWER is:

1. Means by which internat'l actors deal w/ each other
2. Product of tangible materials & intangible behavioral resources

What are the four purposes of "power"?

tangible is concrete MATERIALS; intangible is how nation/agent ACTS

Give examples of tangible vs. intangible resources

3. Means for achieving influence over others
4. Attempt to shape outcome of internat'l events to maintain or improve internat'l political environ.

How does "force" differ from "power"?

~ Power is NOT Force ~ force is at extreme end of continuum of choices available to a nation when agents strive to manipulate outcomes of events.

2" POWER in international relations is when a nation or a leader influences international events via resources. Power has 4 functions; power differs from FORCE, which is extreme manipulation.

[The after-class additions are boxed in the above notes.]

1. *During class,* the student took notes on the six-inch right side of paper.
2. *Soon afterward,* the student went back over notes: clarified terms (*actor, tangible, intangible*) and underlined/highlighted to emphasize key concepts/terms;
3. Created five questions in the "cue column";
4. Covered the notes and recited answers to each question;
5. Wrote a summary in the bottom two-inch space;
6. Reviewed immediately; and then
7. Reflected on the material's overall importance.

try it out!

Target a course in which you take many and frequent class notes. Within 24 hours *after* each class for the next week, review your notes and create a study guide using the strategies illustrated in Figures 4.2, 4.3, 4.4, and 4.5.

Dealing with Difficult Lecturers

igure 4.6 summarizes common difficulties that students encounter in lectures, as well as suggestions for dealing with the difficulties and adapting to instructors' styles. What information can you add?

pause... *and reflect*

Consider the instructors for your classes. Which instructors have exhibited characteristics that you find to be difficult to listen to or distracting? Use Figure 4.6 to identify your instructors' characteristics and accompanying suggestions.

- Which suggestions will you use for that class?
- What *other* suggestions can you add?

Use Figure 4.7 to keep track of suggestions and adaptations for the classes you have identified.

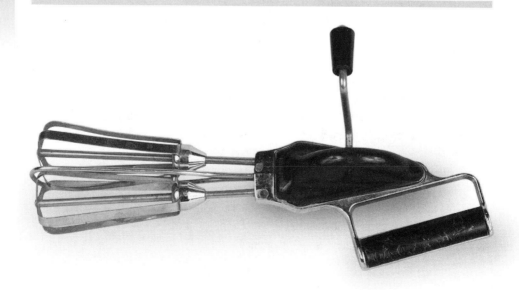

Dealing with difficult lecturers.

FIGURE **4.6**

Instructor Characteristics	Suggestions for Students
Talks over students' heads; uses complex words and ideas.	○ Review chapter to be covered. ○ Ask lots of questions. ○ Talk with the instructor out of class to seek explanations.
Jumps from topic to topic; unorganized.	○ Reorganize notes *after* each class. ○ Have a three-ring binder with the aim of using a separate sheet of paper for each topic; reorganize the pages after class. ○ Leave room within the notes or use the back of the notepaper so you have space to reorganize your notes and fill in details after class. ○ Tape-record (with permission), and use the tape to help you reorganize notes, by topic, after class. ○ Read and review the textbook before and after class to give you background information about organization of topics. ○ Ask lots of questions in and out of class.
Talks too fast.	○ Review notes after every class; use the text to fill in what you missed. ○ Use tape recorder (with permission); listen to the tape after class, and fill in parts you missed. ○ Jot down *only* key points and ideas; leave spaces to fill in added details after class. ○ See the instructor during office hours to review what you missed or don't fully understand. ○ Review notes regularly with other students. ○ Ask the instructor to slow down and/or to repeat information.
Talks with a foreign accent.	○ Sit in the front of the room near the instructor. ○ Talk to the instructor one-on-one; this will help you get used to the professor's manner of speech. ○ Ask the instructor to repeat information. ○ Listen carefully and ask for visual reinforcements, such as the use of overheads, the board, and handouts. ○ Review notes regularly with other students.

(continued)

FIGURE **4.6**   *Continued.*

Instructor Characteristics	Suggestions for Students
Presents information in a lifeless, boring manner.	○ Sit near the instructor. ○ Bring colorful supplies; at least create lively notes for yourself! ○ Ask questions and urge classmates to ask questions to enliven presentation.
Condescending or impersonal toward students.	○ See if you can talk to and form a relationship with the instructor. ○ Ignore it. ○ Seek help and personal affirmation out of class.
Skips over important topics that likely will be on tests.	○ Bring up those topics; ask questions. ○ Ask the instructor to review major topics on the test.
Gives a large amount of information.	○ Dissect information when reviewing notes after class. ○ Go over information in study groups.
Repeats topics too much, or students are too familiar with topics.	○ Ask questions to possibly move the instructor ahead. ○ Ask about related topics. ○ Use markers or colored pens while in class to reinforce and emphasize major concepts within your notes. ○ Look ahead to future topics.
Doesn't want to be bothered explaining material.	○ Be persistent; keep asking questions. ○ Personally talk to the instructor after class to try to establish a working relationship. ○ Seek help from a tutor or another student.
Is unprepared for class.	○ Go to tutoring to fill in gaps. ○ Read and study the textbook before and after class. ○ Ask lots of questions and show interest; this might spur the instructor to better prepare for class.

Others:

Chart for tracking suggestions.

FIGURE 4.7

INSTRUCTOR/SUBJECT	STRATEGIES

try it out!

Learning Style and Active Listening/Note Taking

By combining knowledge, time, and practice, you are developing a system of listening and note taking that is most effective for you. Regularly assess your strategies: Do you need to improve class preparation? Do you want to modify how you listen or where you sit in a particular class? Should you be trying a different format for note taking? By combining the elements of active listening and note taking, with your preferences for learning, you will be able to fine-tune your approaches toward in-class listening and note taking.

1. Write your four-letter "type" (as identified in Chapter 1):

E Extraversion	or	**I**	Introversion,
S Sensing	or	**N**	Intuition,
T Thinking	or	**F**	Feeling, and
J Judging	or	**P**	Perceiving.

2. Using Figure 4.8, find the headings representing your preferences (Extraversion or Introversion, Sensing or Intuition, and Judging or Perceiving), and refer to the left-hand column labeled "Learning Preferences." Consider whether the learning preferences generally describe you.

3. Refer to the corresponding column "Lecture Note-Taking Strategies." Place a check (✓) in the circles next to the strategies that you *do* use regularly.

4. Additionally, if you know whether you prefer to learn using visual, auditory, or kinesthetic/tactile means, take note of those lecture note-taking strategies that are labeled accordingly: Visual = [V], Auditory = [A], Tactile/Kinesthetic = [T/K].

Active listening strategies and learning preferences.   FIGURE **4.8**

LEARNING PREFERENCES* NOTE-TAKING STRATEGIES

Extraversion

- Prefers action and variety.
- Prefers talking to people when doing mental work.
- Likes to clarify ideas out loud.
- Wants to know what others expect of her.

○ Vary the types of study guides you develop from your lecture notes. [T/K]

○ When reviewing your lecture notes, move about [T/K] and recite out loud to yourself [A].

○ Participate in group lecture review sessions. Compare and discuss notes with others. [A]

○ Teach others; this will reinforce what *you know.* [A]

○ Participate in class: ask questions and answer questions. [A]

○ Class lectures and discussion are often your strength; thus (1) go to every class, and (2) use the in-class information as a basis for understanding the course subject matter.

○ If the instructor's expectations are not clear to you, seek out concrete explanations and examples. [T/K]

vs. Introversion

- Prefers to understand something before trying it.

○ Since reading is a strong suit, read the corresponding text material *before* class as a way to strengthen your understanding of the subject matter.

○ Make note of the instructor's in-class questions. Take time after class to think about the correct and complete answers.

○ If appropriate, bring a tape recorder and ask permission to tape the instructor's lecture. After class, use the recording to review those areas within the lecture that you are unsure about. [A]

○ Give yourself reflection time *after* class to reinforce your understanding of main concepts and details.

○ Write down your own questions. [V] [T/K] See the instructor before or after class or during office hours for answers to your questions. [A]

- Prefers to focus on ideas and impressions.
- Has trouble remembering terms and names.

○ Highlight terms and names in class notes. [V]

When you need to know terms and names, go back through your notes after class and create summaries:

○ Make *study cards* with names/terms on front and what they are associated with on back. [V]

○ *Develop a chart* with names and terms in columns and characteristics and other related details in rows. [V]

○ Use *memory tools,* such as mnemonic devices, along with recitation for recall. [A]

○ Create a skit with the terms and names—use zany associations within the skit—and act it out to reinforce remembering. [T/K]   *(continued)*

FIGURE **4.8** *Continued.*

LEARNING PREFERENCES*	NOTE-TAKING STRATEGIES

Sensing

- Prefers using skills already learned.

- Prefers hands-on experiences.
- Prefers to use senses for learning.
- Is patient with details, unless they become too complicated.

○ For each course, establish a *routine* of reviewing lecture notes (either on paper [V] or out loud [A]) at the same days and times each week.

○ Preview (by either reading [V] or reciting [A]) the related text or lab assignment *before* class. This can help you better understand the lecture.

○ When taking notes, write or type details, including facts, examples, and applications. [T/K] Review afterward to make sure your details are correct and that you understand the main concepts.

○ If a laboratory experience is attached to the course, *go.* Take notes, ask questions, and be actively involved. Use the lab experience or a field trip as a basis for understanding and remembering course concepts. [T/K]

○ As you review your notes, fill in *concrete examples* from the text or lab manual. Add *practical applications, effects* or *outcomes,* and *personal experiences* related to the broader theories.

○ Use your *senses* [T/K] when reviewing: recite aloud [A]; move around [T/K]; add visual, colorful emphasis to your notes [V]; participate in a study group in order to discuss and hear others talk about the subject matter [A].

vs. Intuition

- Pays attention to meanings of facts and how they fit together.
- Prefers using imagination; focuses on possibilities.

- Enjoys learning new skills.
- Is impatient with details; doesn't mind complicated situations.

○ Organize and/or summarize class information and notes by developing maps of ideas. [V]

○ *Before* class, skim through the whole chapter, including reading the summary, in order to identify conclusions and see the "whole picture" of the lecture topic. [V]

○ Fill in supporting ideas/details *after* listening for main ideas. [A]

○ Get a study partner or tutor to assist you with routine facts and details. [A]

○ To reduce factual errors, go through text or computer material *after* the lecture to check and add necessary details.

(continued)

Continued.

FIGURE **4.8**

LEARNING PREFERENCES*   **NOTE-TAKING STRATEGIES**

Judging

- Prefers to have a clear understanding and organized plan beforehand.
- Usually has mind made up; may decide things too quickly.

○ Have a set time slot (such as Sunday p.m.) to plan for the week. Look over last week's notes and predict topics for upcoming class sessions and assignments. Prepare a written overview of when to review notes and complete assignments for the week; color-code time slots by subject and/or assignment. [V]

○ Have an organized set of supplies for each subject. Color-code folders and notebooks by subject. [V]

○ Get an overview of the topic *before* class by previewing the chapter, study guide, and/or related assignment.

○ Review lecture notes to see how the information fits into text readings. Talk out loud as you review. [A]

vs. Perceiving

- Prefers to seek new information.
- Decides things slowly.

○ To reduce problems with selecting the key points in a lecture, *review your notes after class;* highlight [V], summarize, or write/type questions that identify the important ideas. [T/K]

○ *Ask questions* in class or in a peer-led study group [A] to satisfy your curiosity and to keep the subject matter interesting and "fresh" for yourself.

○ When listening, make *associations* between new information and familiar experiences; write down the associations, relating the new to the old. [V]

Key   [V]   = Visual
     [A]   = Auditory
     [T/K] = Tactile/Kinesthetic

Source: Learning preferences material from *People Types and Tiger Stripes,* 3rd edition, by Gordon D. Lawrence. Center for Applications of Psychological Type, Gainesville, FL, 1993. Used with permission. This exercise is NOT a type indicator, nor does it replicate the Myers-Briggs Type Indicator® which is a validated instrument.

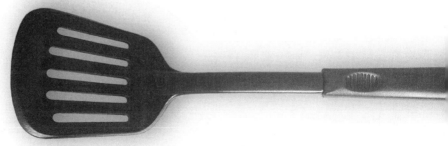

try it out!

Identify a specific strategy that you will try *this week*. Using Figure 4.10, write a Personal Action Statement for that strategy. Refer to the examples in Figure 4.9 for suggestions. At the end of the week, **Assess Your Success:**

- Did you follow through and reward yourself accordingly?
- Did the hurdle materialize, and did you manage it effectively?
- Examine your habits *before*, *during*, and *after* a class. Do you need to make any additional changes?

FIGURE **4.9**   *Examples of students' personal action statements.*

1. I will: _reduce daydreaming during my history class._
2. My greatest hurdle to achieving this is: _I get bored during class._
3. I will eliminate this hurdle by: _(1) participating more during class— asking at least one question each class session; and (2) reviewing class material with my classmate Lisa each week._
4. My time frame for achieving this is: _I will begin during tomorrow's class and evaluate when I meet with Lisa each week._
5. My reward for achieving this is: _Feeling like I'm not wasting my time during this class. Also, hopefully I'll be rewarded with a higher grade on my next quiz._

1. I will: _highlight important ideas in my philosophy notes after each class._
2. My greatest hurdle to achieving this is: _to go back to my room after class to check my e-mail._
3. I will eliminate this hurdle by: _reviewing my notes for 15–20 minutes while I get a cup of coffee and THEN going back to my room._
4. My time frame for achieving this is: _to begin after my next philosophy class on Wed._
5. My reward for achieving this is: _checking my e-mail IF I review my notes. I'll see if this motivates me during the next week._

Your personal action statement.   FIGURE **4.10**

1. I will: _____
   _____
   _____

2. My greatest hurdle to achieving this is: _____
   _____
   _____

3. I will eliminate this hurdle by: _____
   _____
   _____
   _____

4. My time frame for achieving this is: _____
   _____

5. My reward for achieving this is: _____
   _____
   _____

"I know reviewing class notes is important for learning. However, with a husband, a full-time job, two aging parents, not to mention household duties, I've always had problems finding the time. However, lately I've done two things that have greatly helped:

1. Between classes, I review what happened by talking (silently) to myself.

2. When in the car, I review by listening to a tape of the day's lecture."
   —KYLIE

STUDENT VOICES

Conclusion

As your classes vary, so will your listening and note-taking techniques. New subjects and different instructors will spur you to alter how you best listen, take notes, and study for each course. As you assess and modify strategies, take into account this checklist of basic ingredients for successful class listening and note taking.

KEY ELEMENTS OF EFFECTIVE LISTENING AND NOTE TAKING

Do . . .

- Go to all classes.
- Come rested and fed.
- Bring appropriate supplies: notebook paper and pens/pencils/highlighters.
- Be familiar with the material to be covered in class.
- Sit in front, near the instructor and away from distractions.
- Listen actively; select ideas to write down on notepaper or type on computer.
- Create notes that are concise, clear, and correct.
- Be alert; write/type, participate, and consciously *want* to pay attention.
- Adapt to your instructor's style and expectations.
- Review your notes *soon* after class while creating a study guide for yourself.

Don't . . .

- Write/type *every word* your instructor says or *only* words you see on the board.
- Copy classmates' notes or purchase ready-made notes in lieu of taking your own notes.
- Gripe about your instructor and complain about the class. Instead, put your energies toward positive outcomes by obtaining class information, completing assignments, and preparing for tests.

CHAPTER 5

Reading and Studying Textbooks

FOCUS QUESTIONS

How can I better *understand* and *remember* what I read?

What are several recommended strategies *before*, *during*, and *after* reading?

Why is each strategy important?

CHAPTER TERMS

After reading the chapter, define (in your own words) and provide an example for each of the following terms:

- closed-ended question words
- idea map
- open-ended question words
- previewing
- summary chart
- timeline
- visual study guide

Understanding and Remembering: The Essential Ingredients

Can you identify with the following student?

Ted has to read Chapter 5 in the *Introduction to Psychology* textbook before tomorrow's class. He opens his text to the beginning of Chapter 5 and then flips to the end to see how many pages the chapter is. To his dismay, the chapter is 30 pages long! He gets out his blue highlighter pen and highlights sentences and paragraphs that, as his eyes move across the page, he thinks are important. He reaches the end of the chapter about an hour later. "Whew, I'm done with that assignment," Ted thinks as he contentedly closes his textbook, expecting to reopen it three weeks from now when he will reread all the blue sections of the pages in preparation for the midterm exam.

However, if someone were to ask Ted to summarize what he just read about in Chapter 5, he could not do it. In fact, the next day in the psychology lecture, Ted was not at all familiar with the terms and ideas that the professor was talking about, even though this material was covered in Chapter 5 of the text. In reality, all Ted accomplished the night before was to create 30 blue pages! He had no understanding, let alone recall, of the important ideas presented in the text chapter.

Ted's method for reading the text material is all too universal. Many students feel a sense of accomplishment with getting the task done, that is, going through the pages, without obtaining a true understanding of what they are reading. If you fall into that category, strategies for reading and studying do exist that can increase both your understanding *and* recall of important information. These strategies are suitable and adaptable for traditional textbooks, novels, and articles as well as electronic books and web-based reading assignments.

pause... *and reflect*

Describe yourself as a reader—that is, characterize your usual approach to a reading assignment. Consider these points:

YOUR READING *BEHAVIORS*—WHAT YOU DO WHEN YOU HAVE AN ASSIGNMENT

- Do you tend to read the assignment immediately or to procrastinate?
- Do you prepare or organize yourself *before* reading? For instance, do you skim through the assignment or look at the end-of-chapter questions or number of pages?

- As you read, what do you do? Do you read the whole assignment at one sitting, or do you take frequent breaks? Do you write in your textbook? Do you highlight, take separate notes, or answer study guide questions?
- Are you able to *concentrate* when reading? How do you keep your mind focused?
- *Afterward*, do you review what you read? Do you reread the entire assignment? Do you quiz yourself?

YOUR *ATTITUDE* TOWARD READING ASSIGNMENTS

- Are you generally *motivated* to begin the assignment?
- Do you *persist*, even if you think the content is boring or difficult to understand?
- Do you often *avoid* reading? Do you *dislike* reading? Why?

YOUR *LEARNING STYLES*, OR *PREFERENCES*, WHEN READING

- When reading, do you prefer complete *silence*, or do you prefer *music* or *background noise?*
- How long can you read and still maintain your *focus:* 10 minutes, a half an hour, or how long? How about breaks? Do you need to *move around* frequently when reading? Do you tend to *move your mouth* or "hear" yourself read?
- When reading, do you concentrate best at a particular *location* and *time of day?*

The following ingredients are essential for understanding and remembering what you read:

1. Preview what's ahead.
2. Break up your reading.
3. Create study guides.
4. Review periodically.

Preview What's Ahead

Previewing will help you learn new, and often complex, information contained in reading assignments. Previewing means getting a quick picture of the "whole" before proceeding with the detailed "parts" of a chapter or article. The more familiar you are with any subject or idea, the more likely you will understand it. Familiarize yourself with both the topic and the layout of the assignment. The previewing step is a way to build a strong, familiar framework for understanding and remembering new material. In addition, the few minutes you spend previewing can greatly improve your concentration while reading.

GET AN OVERVIEW OF THE BOOK

What parts of a textbook can you glance at in order to become familiar with the content? The Table of Contents is important because it presents the overall organization of the book. Also, skim through the Preface, Introduction, Copyright, Index, Appendices, and Answer Keys. You need only do this step once: before you begin reading the first chapter assignment. This quick initial step will provide you with a general idea of the overall layout of the text, the organization of content, the author's viewpoint, and any text-related aids to assist you when reading.

try it out!

Preview a textbook that you are using this term. After previewing, you should be able to answer these questions:

- What are the key components of the text?
- What is the general organization of content?
- How difficult does the text seem to be?
- What related guides, CDs, or web pages are available?

GET AN OVERVIEW OF THE CHAPTER OR ARTICLE

You want to gain some familiarity with a chapter or article that you are about to read. Previewing means flipping through pages and glancing at the characteristics of the chapter, including headings, subheadings, introductions, summaries, questions, length, vocabulary/terminology, graphics, spacing, and overall layout. Once you are acquainted with the topics, organization, and difficulty level of the chapter/article, you are prepared to read for both understanding and recall.

try it out!

To understand the benefits of previewing, open your text to a new chapter. Allow yourself *one minute* to flip through the pages and note characteristics of the chapter, such as the headings, subheadings, questions, summary, and so on. At the end of one minute, close the text and recite to yourself what you just found out about the chapter. Nothing is too insignificant to note.

You likely will recall information about the chapter's topics and content as well as details about the format, such as the length, graphics, and difficulty

level. Most students are surprised about how much information can be gleaned from a chapter in a minute; this information provides you with a familiar context from which to begin your reading of the assignment.

IDENTIFY YOUR PURPOSE

Why are you reading this chapter? *What* are you going to do with the information? Your purpose for reading helps you identify how much and what type of information you need to know. If your purpose is to use the information for class discussion, you only need to read to understand the main concepts in the chapter. If your purpose is to do well on the upcoming 100-point test, you will need to read for main ideas as well as for lots of supporting ideas and details. A 10-point quiz on the chapter content means that you will need to read primarily for main ideas. Be clear about what type of questions you will be asked and how much detail you are expected to know. Thus, for peak reading efficiency, be clear as to *why* you are reading and *how much* information you need to know.

Break Up Your Reading

For maximum effectiveness, read *one section* of a chapter or article at a time. Reading a section at a time makes sense because the author has already divided the material into paragraphs around a common topic; therefore, take advantage of these divisions. After reading the section, stop and ask yourself: "What are the key ideas?" If you honestly cannot identify the important ideas, go back and reread the section.

Sometimes reading an entire section at once is too much. If the material is difficult and complicated, you might need to read a paragraph at a time to fully understand the subject matter. Or, if the section is quite long, you may need to divide it up and read several paragraphs before stopping and checking for comprehension. However, do not break up your reading into chunks that are too small. Not only can it become tedious and time consuming to stop after every paragraph, but frequent stops can chop up ideas to the point that the material doesn't flow and, ultimately, doesn't make sense to you.

Create Study Guides

Combining *reading* with *studying* is an effective and efficient technique. Unlike Ted, described at the beginning of this chapter, do not separate the two. Instead, as you read, *think* and *write*. After reading a section, stop and ask yourself: What did I just read about? What's important for me to know about this topic? Then, write your answers. The following suggestions will guide you in selecting important points as you read.

1. Focus on *major events or concepts*, noting:
    *   *Significant changes* that developed as a result of these events/concepts.
    *   *Connections* between these events/concepts.
    *   *Distinguishing characteristics* of these events/concepts.
    *   *Key individuals* associated with these events/concepts.

2. Identify *key words* or *terms*.
    *   *Paraphrase*, in your own words, what they mean.
    *   Add *examples* that help you explain or understand the term.

By writing down important points, you will be (1) immediately reinforcing the information, and (2) developing a study guide for later review.

STEPS FOR EFFECTIVELY AND EFFICIENTLY READING AN ASSIGNMENT

1. *Preview* to obtain a general idea of what's ahead.
2. *Read* a section.

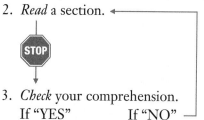

3. *Check* your comprehension.
    If "YES"   If "NO"
4. *Create* your study guide.
5. *Review* periodically in order to remember.

You have choices as to the type of study guide you can create. Your decision depends on your purpose for reading, your background and familiarity with the subject, the difficulty level of the text, your learning preferences, and what you need to know for the upcoming quiz, exam, or discussion. The purpose of a study guide is to help you

*   select,
*   organize,
*   understand, and
*   remember key information for your course.

An effective study guide presents information in an organized, concise manner and helps you learn and recall text information. The intent of a study guide is to maximize both the *effectiveness* and the *efficiency* by which you study for your courses. Types of study guides that are useful for college students are described on the following pages.

QUESTION-AND-ANSWER STUDY GUIDE

Three words that are key to increasing your reading comprehension and concentration are *what*, *why*, and *how*. These are termed **open-ended question words** because they generate answers that are broader and more conceptual in nature than do the other three question words: *who*, *when*, and *where*. The answers to *what*, *why*, and *how* tend to be *main ideas*. On the other hand, the answers to *who*, *when*, and *where* tend to be *specific facts*, which is the reason they are termed **closed-ended question words.**

For the question-and-answer study guide, you develop questions to guide your reading; that is, you *read to discover the answers to questions*. If the chapter or article that you are reading contains headings, use the headings as a basis for creating questions. Otherwise, create your own questions. In order to focus on main ideas and concepts, use *what*, *why*, and *how* questions. If you need to know details for tests, add *who*, *when*, and *where* questions. After reading a section, think about—and write—the answer to each question. Write your question and accompanying answer in the textbook, on a separate sheet of paper, or on index cards for later self-testing.

Figure 5.1 provides an example of study guide questions created from chapter headings. By creating questions and then answering the questions, you will

Example of study guide questions. FIGURE **5.1**

1. heading: The Steps of the Scientific Method
   question: What are the steps of the scientific method?

2. heading: Forming a Hypothesis
   question: How should I form a hypothesis?

3. heading: The Importance of Observation
   question: Why is observation an important part of the scientific method?

4. heading: The Baroque Era of Music
   questions: What are the major characteristics of baroque music?
              Who were the major composers during the era?
              When did the baroque period begin and end?

be actively identifying important ideas within a section and thus becoming a more focused reader. In addition, you will have developed a question-and-answer study guide for later review.

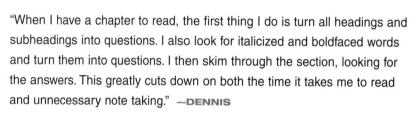

"I used to just jump in and read. Now, I begin by reading the introduction and conclusion; this gives me a general idea of what I will be reading. Also, I change headings into questions and try to answer those questions to see how much I comprehend. These are the best habits that I've gotten into."
—SHI-ANN

"When I have a chapter to read, the first thing I do is turn all headings and subheadings into questions. I also look for italicized and boldfaced words and turn them into questions. I then skim through the section, looking for the answers. This greatly cuts down on both the time it takes me to read and unnecessary note taking." —DENNIS

HIGHLIGHTING-PLUS-MARKING STUDY GUIDE

The advantage of highlighting and underlining is that you can emphasize important ideas in the text without rewriting the ideas on a separate sheet of paper. Consider the following factors when highlighting.

1. **Read first; then highlight.** If you highlight *as* you read, it is difficult to distinguish important ideas from unimportant ideas. Also, because ideas are often repeated within a section, you tend to overhighlight if you don't read the material first. In addition, highlighting while you read can disrupt concentration. Instead, read the section first, and then use highlighting as a means to *check your understanding* of key ideas.

2. **Highlight as little as possible to get the idea across.** Most students err on the side of overhighlighting—that is, they think nearly everything is important. This defeats the purpose of a study guide; if you emphasize too much, you end up rereading most of the chapter or article. Instead, focus on *key words or phrases* that get the idea across. Avoid highlighting whole sentences or, worse yet, whole paragraphs. If everything in a paragraph is noteworthy, use markings in the margins to emphasize *what* and *why* the information is important.

The advantage of adding markings on a page is that you are not limited to just the words used in the text. Markings help make important ideas clearer and more distinct. Such markings include:

Example of highlighting-plus-marking.   FIGURE **5.2**

visual learn'g preferences

Bio. Prof.
Dr. Ada Worth is a visual learner and, therefore, relies on visual strategies and
3 ex. of tchng. strategies
materials when teaching her biology classes. For lectures, she writes most of the
(1)   (2)
ideas on the board and often uses the overhead projector. Also, she gives students
(3)   3 ex. of student expectations
handouts illustrating material covered in each class. Furthermore, she wants
(1)
students to use the mapping format of note taking to summarize articles discussed
(2)
in class. Finally, she expects students to keep their lab areas free of clutter and to

write neat, clear notes in their lab manuals.

* How am I a visual lrner??

- *Summarizing* a passage with a short phrase [EX: "visual learn'g preferences"].
- Indicating the *organization* of material [EX: (1) (2) (3)].
- Using *symbols* to *emphasize* ideas [EX: +, >, ——➤, *].
- Indicating *why* ideas are important to know [EX: "How am I a visual learner?"].

Markings combined with highlighting or underlining is an effective study guide because you are *interacting* with the text material, making ideas as explicit as possible. See Figure 5.2 for an example of a highlighting-plus-marking study guide.

"I *never* marked books—it was not allowed. Even today, if I make a stray mark or accidentally bend a page, I am appalled at my own carelessness! I recently realized that my attitude needs to change if I am to survive as a college student; I am learning to value books in a different way. Lately, I've been underlining important ideas, and so far the book hasn't self-destructed!" —**NICOLE**

"In the past, textbook reading seemed a waste of time. I would think: "Why read the textbook when the professor gives us notes?" However, it was impossible for me to excel this way, so I started reading and highlighting. At first I was highlighting *everything* in the chapter. I was reading chapters two or three times because I thought everything was important, which is why I got bored when reading. Since then, I have highlighted *words,* not entire sentences. This has helped me to slow down and more precisely understand what I am reading. Also, I discovered that marking in the margins makes the important points stand out so that they catch my eye." —**GAVIN**

"Often, the class material and book material are parallel. Thus I read the chapter *before* class so that I can more easily keep up with the instructor's lecture. I bring my book notes to class and mark in the margins what the instructor goes over so I know what to study for a test. I always mark examples used in class; examples make great memory joggers in the middle of a "blank out" during a test. In addition, if I have a question in class, I see if I can answer it myself by first referring to my book notes." —**KATIE**

OUTLINING STUDY GUIDE

You likely are familiar with the standard format for outlining a passage: organizing notes by writing main ideas to the left with supporting ideas underneath, indenting to the right as ideas become less general and more detailed. Outlining is most effective if you paraphrase ideas presented in the text, that is, if you write—or type—key points in *your own words,* adding explanations or examples. In Figure 5.3, note the use of "action words" to begin the phrases in the outline.

Example of outlining.   FIGURE   5.3

Dr. Ada Worth is a visual learner and therefore relies on visual strategies and materials when teaching her biology classes. For lectures, she writes most of the ideas on the board and often uses the overhead projector. Also, she gives students handouts illustrating material covered in each class. She wants students to use the mapping format of note taking to summarize articles discussed in class. Finally, she expects students to keep their lab areas free of clutter and to write neat, clear notes in their lab manuals.

I. Dr. Worth ⟶ visual lrnr./instructor
   A. Lecture techniques
      1. Writes on board
      2. Uses overhead projector
   B. Provides handouts
   C. Uses mapping
   D. Lab expectations
      1. Neat environment
      2. Neat student notes

STUDY CARDS

Study cards are especially effective when you need to know *terms* and *definitions*, including examples and applications of the term. The front of an index card showcases a name, term, concept, or main idea. Putting the term or idea in a question format helps you focus on what you need to know. For instance, if you are reading about the scientific method, on the front of your study card write "What are steps of the scientific method?" On the back, write the definition, explanation, example, or other appropriate details. Be concise and use your own words.

An advantage of study cards is that you must be *selective* when reading a text since you are separating text information into individual parts for the front and back of the cards. Study cards can help you pinpoint main ideas and related details in the text. In addition, study cards are excellent tools for orally quizzing yourself and teaching others. Create study cards if you want *repetitive* reinforcement of text information.

FIGURE **5.4**   *Examples of study cards.*

FRONTS

What are <u>sedimentary</u> rocks?

Why important?

What are <u>metamorphic</u> rocks?

Why important?

BACKS

— Made of particles; fragments cemented together.

— Gives clues to ancient environment & climates.

— Any igneous or sed. rock that is burned; changes form.

— Gives clues about plate tectonics.

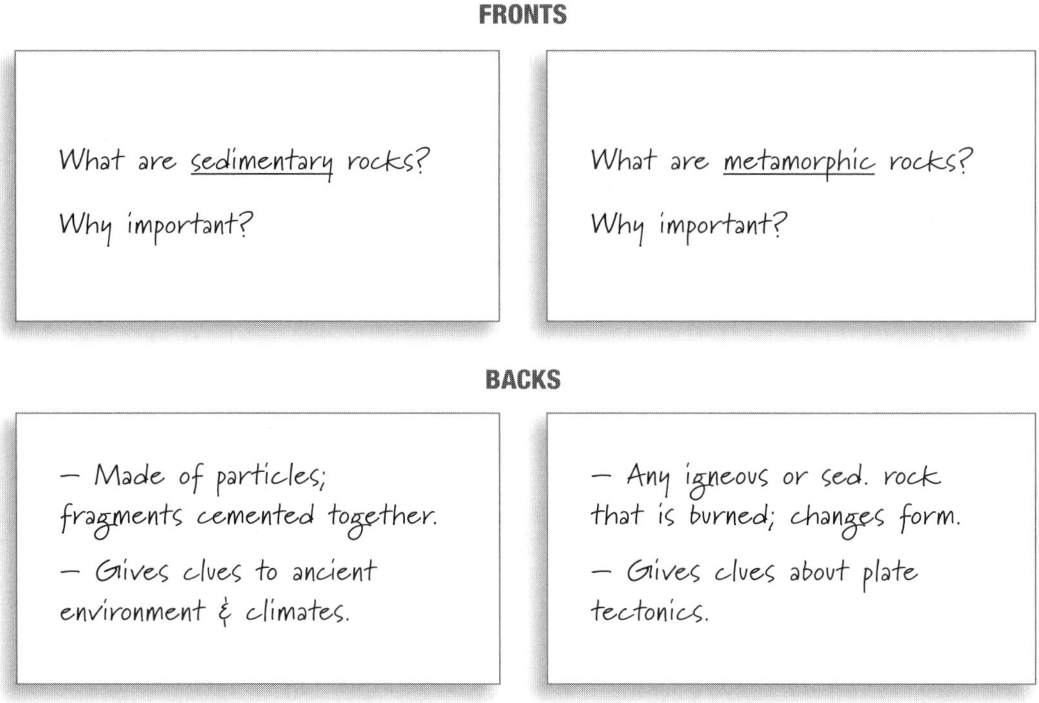

However, a disadvantage of study cards is the tendency for students to memorize, as opposed to learn, the information. Study cards generally are *not* effective for in-depth analysis and synthesis of text material. Figure 5.4 shows two examples of study cards.

VISUAL STUDY GUIDES: MAPS, SUMMARY CHARTS, AND TIMELINES

Most people learn and recall best when they can visualize information. Idea maps, summary charts, and timelines are all visual summaries of ideas in print. A **visual study guide** involves *active reading* of text material in order to

1. Identify *key* ideas—both major and minor—in the text passage.
2. Identify *relationships* among these ideas.
3. Create an organized, concise *summary*.

Reading to "fill in" a map, chart, or timeline can be an efficient method of reading a text. First, identify the overall relationships among ideas in the passage and create a "frame" for your chart or map. By first recognizing the categories or type of information you need to know, you will be eliminating unneeded information when reading the text. Then read to complete the study guide. This technique of reading to fill in a chart, map, or timeline can speed up your reading and thus is an efficient reading strategy.

Furthermore, visual guides are excellent tools to use for review before exams. In order to create a visual study guide, you will be organizing, categorizing, and simplifying text information, all of which result in *knowing* the material. The concise, visual image provides a perfect format for speedy overviews before a test. A number of computer programs are available that enable you to create visual study guides.

Models of visual study guides include the following:

- **Idea maps** (Figure 5.5) are especially appropriate for showing the *connections* among *main ideas* and *subordinate supporting ideas.*

Four examples of idea maps.   FIGURE **5.5**

I. The topic (*1960s Protest Movements*) is divided into *three* **main ideas,** each of which has offshoots—**supporting ideas** with **details.** Note the parallel placement of the supporting ideas with similar themes: (1) which phase of the movement, and (2) people.

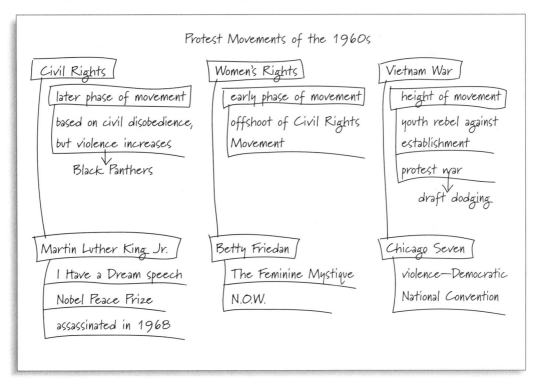

Protest Movements of the 1960s

Civil Rights
- later phase of movement
- based on civil disobedience, but violence increases
  - Black Panthers

Women's Rights
- early phase of movement
- offshoot of Civil Rights Movement

Vietnam War
- height of movement
- youth rebel against establishment
- protest war
  - draft dodging

Martin Luther King Jr.
- I Have a Dream speech
- Nobel Peace Prize
- assassinated in 1968

Betty Friedan
- The Feminine Mystique
- N.O.W.

Chicago Seven
- violence—Democratic National Convention

FIGURE **5.5**   *Four examples of idea maps, continued.*

II. The **topic** (*"STUDY CARDS for reading"*) is divided into two distinct **categories** (*"ADVANTAGES"* and *"DISADVANTAGES"*).

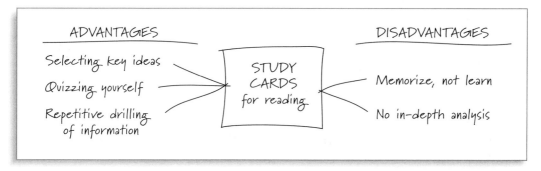

III. This idea map presents the two parts ("active" vs. "inactive") related to the topic ("quiet breathing").

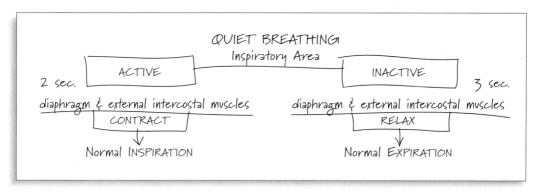

IV. This idea map illustrates a **cause and effect** relationship among ideas. The topic is "The Industrial Revolution."

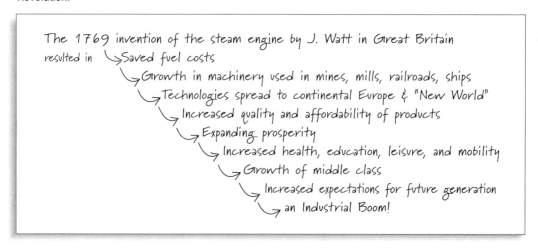

- **Summary charts** (Figure 5.6) present an effective *framework* for *summarizing* and *categorizing key features*, including definitions, characteristics, accompanying examples, and relationships.
- **Timelines** (Figure 5.7) are suitable for material organized in *chronological order*, such as a progression of events or steps in a process.

Two examples of summary charts.   FIGURE 5.6

PSYCHOLOGICAL DISORDERS

TYPES	DEFINITION	EXAMPLES	FEELINGS
Anxiety	Characterized by distressing, persistent anxiety	1) Panic attacks—last several minutes; intense dread 2) Phobias—fears	Chest pain, choking, smothering sensation, rapid heart beat
Somatoform	Symptoms take solo form w/ no physical cause	1) Conversion disorder—anxiety is converted into 2) Hypochondria—interrupts normal sensations	Dizziness, vomiting, blurred vision
Dissociative	Conscious awareness becomes separated from memories	1) Amnesia—failure to recall events 2) Fugue—fleeing one's home & identity for days/months	Facing trauma, forgot what was intolerable or painful, the way they should act or feel
Mood	Emotional extremes	1) Major depression—prolonged depression 2) Bipolar disorder—alternates between depression and mania	Lack of energy, not able to eat/sleep normally, feeling of being better off dead; much pressure

FIGURE **5.6**   *Two examples of summary charts, continued.*

Cause-and-Effect Chart for Civil Rights Movement

CAUSE	EFFECT
Southern closed society	- Blacks excluded from politics - Whites controlled economy - Segregation is the norm
13th amendment	- Ends slavery
14th amendment	- Nobody can be processed without due process
15th amendment	- Black men allowed to vote
Jim Crow laws	- Revokes blacks of all their rights
Plessy vs. Ferguson 1896	- Establishes doctrine "separate but equal"
Black soldiers returning from WWII	- Demanded jobs (learned skills during war) and desegregation
Brown vs. Board of Education (1954)	- Most important civil rights case - Ruled unanimously that "separate but equal" is not equal
Southern Manifesto	- 100 congressmen oppose desegregation - Say it violates the Constitution and the 14th amendment
Montgomery bus boycott	- Strong black community - MLK Jr. put into national role - Combination of legal strategies and nonviolent direct action - Protest begins the movement - SCLC is formed

[created by Melissa Swope]

Two examples of timelines.   FIGURE **5.7**

Feminist Movement

Time Period: Goals, Accomplishments, & Characteristics:

| 1st Wave | 1848–1950s |

1. 1848: Start of Women's Suffrage Movement. Delegates to Women's Rights Convention, Seneca Falls, NY, adopted Declaration of Sentiments. 1st public demand for women's independ. Supporters insulted, assaulted, &/or ignored by pop. press & leaders.
2. 1900: Suffragists publicly marched protesting for right to vote.
3. 1920: Women received right to vote.
4. Break from women's traditional roles of dependency & submission.

| 2nd Wave | 1960s–1980s |

1. Women's continuing social, legal, & financial independence & self-direction.
2. Enlightenment of options in & out of home.
3. "Equal Pay for Equal Work."
4. Opening doors in nontraditional workplaces.
5. Reproductive choices & freedoms.
6. Primarily involved white, middle-class women.

| 3rd Wave | 1990s–21st Century |

1. Breaking the "glass ceiling" to top positions within workplaces.
2. Addressing race & class inequalities.
3. Overcoming domestic violence & rape.
4. Rights of homosexuals & transgendered people.
5. Broadening scope of feminism.
6. Focus feminism on daily practicality, as opposed to theory & intellectuality.

FIGURE **5.7** *Two examples of timelines, continued.*

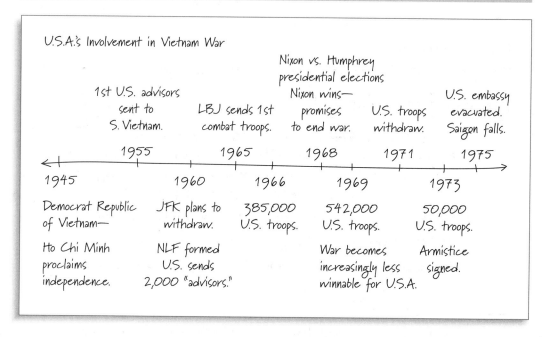

U.S.A.'s Involvement in Vietnam War

Review Periodically

 t least once a week, look over your study guide. This regular review keeps the many and varied pieces of information rooted in your memory. Here are some suggested approaches for weekly review.

ADD OR COMBINE LECTURE MATERIAL

Are there parts of the text that help to clarify complex ideas from the lecture or vice versa? Can you identify overlapping text and lecture information—information that likely will be on a future exam? Can you "see" how parts of the text and lecture relate to one another and combine to form an image of the whole?

TALK ALOUD

As you review, say the information aloud, either to yourself or to another person. Use as many of your senses as possible to learn and remember the new information—*see* the information in your study guide, *say* the information aloud, and *hear* yourself, thus reinforcing the subject matter. If possible, *teach* someone else as you review; find a friend, classmate, or family member who will listen and ask questions as you explain the information. If you can clearly *teach* it to another person, you likely *know* it.

ANTICIPATE TEST QUESTIONS

Predict and write down questions you expect to be on the upcoming quiz or exam. This tactic will help you be selective with quantities of information. Also, you will be thinking of the information in terms of immediate use, that is, *knowing it for the test.*

try it out!

Using your current course assignments, create and use the various types of study guides. After using each study guide, **Assess Your Success** by writing its advantages and disadvantages on Figure 5.8. Use the following four questions to guide you as you judge the value and drawbacks of each type of study guide.

GUIDELINES FOR ASSESSING A STUDY GUIDE

1. Does this study guide help me *understand* the content as I read?
2. Does this study guide help keep my attention *focused* on what I am reading?
3. Does this study guide help me *remember* important information?
4. Is this study guide a worthwhile tool for *review* before a test?

Assessing study guides.   FIGURE **5.8**

Study Guide	Advantages	Disadvantages
Question and Answer		
Highlighting plus Marking		
Outlining		
Study Cards		
Idea Map		
Summary Chart		
Timeline		

try it out!

Learning Style and Reading/Studying Strategies

The following pages contain charts linking learning styles with reading strategies. You will select, implement, and assess a specific strategy that matches your learning preference.

1. Write your four-letter "type" (as identified in Chapter 1):

E Extraversion	or	**I** Introversion,
S Sensing	or	**N** Intuition,
T Thinking	or	**F** Feeling, and
J Judging	or	**P** Perceiving.

2. Using Figure 5.9, circle the headings representing your preferences (Extraversion or Introversion, Sensing or Intuition, and Judging or Perceiving), and refer to the left-hand column labeled "Learning Preferences." Do the characteristics generally describe you when you are reading and studying?

3. Refer to the corresponding column "Reading and Studying Strategies." Place a check (✓) in the circles next to the strategies that you *do* use *regularly*.

4. If you know your preferences for either visual, auditory, or tactile/kinesthetic learning modes, take note of those reading and studying strategies that are labeled accordingly: Visual = [V], Auditory = [A], Tactile/Kinesthetic = [T/K].

Reading and studying strategies and learning preferences.   FIGURE **5.9**

LEARNING PREFERENCES*   READING AND STUDYING STRATEGIES

Extraversion

- Prefers action and variety.

  ○ Read for short chunks of time, taking regular breaks in which you move about. [T/K]

  ○ Vary the *types* of study guides you develop for reading. Use a variety of colors and designs. [V]

  ○ Move your fingers across the page as you read. [T/K]

  ○ Pace around the room as you read, or "act out" what you are reading. [T/K]

  ○ *To speed up your reading:* (1) focus on the first and last sentences of paragraphs; (2) use chapter headings as guides to identify main ideas; (3) create a study guide by turning headings into questions; then read to answer the questions.

- Prefers talking when doing mental work.

  ○ Compare/contrast your study guides with others. [A]

  ○ Participate in group study and review sessions to *discuss* text information. [A]

  ○ Teach others; this will reinforce what *you* know about subjects. [A]

- Acts quickly, sometimes with little reflection.

  ○ Use a simple question-and-answer (*what, how, why, who, when, where*) study guide for text reading. This will expedite your reading while focusing your attention on important ideas.

  ○ Class lectures/discussions are often your strength, so use class information as a basis for understanding the text. [A]

- Wants to know what other people's expectations are.

  ○ Be clear regarding how text information is used in class discussion—what do you need to know for the upcoming exams?

vs. Introversion

- Prefers to understand something before trying.
- Prefers to understand the idea of a task.
- Reading is a strength in learning.

  ○ When reading, *focus on main ideas first* (that is, look at the first and last sentences; read the summary) to understand the "big picture." Then, go back and read more carefully for details. [V]

  ○ Your preferences are an advantage in developing a thorough text study guide, such as highlighting *and* marking.

  ○ You often see relationships among text ideas; thus, create an *idea map* relating main ideas with details. Or, develop a *chart* that illustrates key names/terms and accompanying characteristics or details. [V]

- Prefers setting own standards.

  ○ Create a plan of when, where, and how you will read assignments. [V]

(continued)

FIGURE **5.9** *Continued.*

LEARNING PREFERENCES*   READING AND STUDYING STRATEGIES

Sensing

- Pays attention to experience and to what something *is*.

  - ○ Master a reading technique and *stick with it.*
  - ○ For each course, set up a regular day/time/place in which to read assignments.

- Prefers using skills already learned more than learning new skills.

  - ○ Use *conventional, familiar* formats for study guides, such as highlighting and marking, outlining, or using review cards. [V] [T/K] Talk as you write. [A]

- Is patient with routine details, but impatient when details become complicated.

  - ○ First focus on details in your reading; then work toward identifying main ideas.
  - ○ Develop *detailed study guides,* such as highlighting and marking, outlining, and using study cards. [V] [T/K] Talk as you write. [A]
  - ○ Use already-made text study guides and/or answer chapter questions.

vs. Intuition

- Likes solving new problems; dislikes doing the same thing over and over.

  - ○ View reading as a *discovery of new ideas.*

- Is impatient with details; is patient with complicated situations.

  - ○ Organize text information by developing idea maps, charts, or timelines of ideas. [V]
  - ○ Obtain an overview of the reading assignment in order to see the whole: preread the introduction, headings, and summary. [V]
  - ○ Get a study partner or tutor to assist you with details. [A]
  - ○ Fill in supporting ideas/details *after* you've read for the main ideas.

(continued)

try it out!

Identify one strategy that would help you when you read and study. Using Figure 5.10, write a Personal Action Statement showing how you will apply that strategy when reading your next assignment.

After completing the strategy, refer back to your Personal Action Statement and **Assess Your Success:**

- Did you accomplish what you set out to do?
- Were you able to overcome any obstacles?

Continued.
FIGURE **5.9**

LEARNING PREFERENCES*	READING AND STUDYING STRATEGIES

Judging

- Likes to get things settled.
  - ○ Get an overview *before* reading: look at headings and summaries. [V] If desired, say it out loud. [A]
- May decide things too quickly.
  - ○ Review lecture notes before reading in order to see how class information fits into text readings.

vs. Perceiving

- May have trouble making decisions.
  - ○ To reduce problems with selecting important points, *review text information after class*—highlight, summarize, or write questions that identify key ideas. [V] [T/K]
  - ○ To confirm your selection of key ideas, review text information with a peer tutor or others in a study group. [A]
- Tends to be curious.
  - ○ Write questions alongside your reading. [T/K]
  - ○ Make associations between new information and familiar experiences—as you read, jot down the associations, relating the new to the old. [T/K]

Key   [V]   = Visual
      [A]   = Auditory
      [T/K] = Tactile/Kinesthetic

Source: Learning preferences material from *People Types and Tiger Stripes,* 3rd edition, by Gordon D. Lawrence. Center for Applications of Psychological Type, Gainesville, FL, 1993. Used with permission. This exercise is NOT a type indicator, nor does it replicate the Myers-Briggs Type Indicator® which is a validated instrument.

- Think about your experience and how successful you were with understanding and remembering what you read. What additional behaviors or different techniques can you implement to make your system of reading and study effective and efficient for *you?* Incorporate these new strategies into a Personal Action Statement for your next reading assignment.

FIGURE **5.10** *Your personal action statement.*

Identify a reading assignment: _____

1. I will: _____

_____

_____

_____

2. My greatest hurdle to achieving this is: _____

_____

_____

_____

3. I will eliminate this hurdle by: _____

_____

_____

_____

4. My time frame for achieving this is: _____

_____

_____

5. My reward for achieving this is: _____

_____

_____

_____

Conclusion

BEFORE YOU READ

- **Know *why* you are reading the material.** What are you going to *do* with
  the information? Are you taking a short quiz, a longer exam, or an essay
  test, or is this information for class discussion? Tailor your reading to fit
  the purpose of each assignment.

- **Get an *overview* of the chapter or article.**
  - *Skim over* headings, italicized and boldfaced print, the introduction, the summary, and the questions at the end.
  - Note the *order* and *difficulty* level of material.
  - Anticipate *how long* you will need to read for an understanding of the information.

DURING YOUR READING

- ***Break up* your reading.** Reading in *small chunks* of time helps keep your concentration high and your mind focused.
- ***Think* about what is important to know.** If you read to *discover ideas,* you will increase your understanding of the material.
- ***Create* a study guide.** This should reflect what you *need to know* for the upcoming exam or discussion.

"Surveying helps me see what the author is trying to teach. I make my own questions and try to answer them; this helps keep me interested in the reading. Reciting my answers helps me know if I really understand what I am reading. Constant review has saved me from forgetting (which I'm a real expert at doing). Reviewing keeps the subject fresh and pulls the main ideas together to give an overview of what the author is expressing." —**PATRICE**

STUDENT VOICES

AFTER YOU READ

- ***Review* your study guides weekly.**
  - Review the text with the lecture.
  - Talk aloud.
  - Anticipate test questions.

See Figure 5.11 for a summary of study guides.

FIGURE **5.11**   *Summary of study guides.*

Description	Advantages	Disadvantages
QUESTIONS AND ANSWERS		
Develop questions from headings/subheadings; Then *read to discover the answers.*	• Predicting questions will increase your reading comprehension. • *What, why, how* questions direct your attention to *key ideas,* thus increasing concentration while reading. • You tend to read faster; thus, is beneficial for a *large amount* of reading.	• By reading *just* to answer a question, you could be missing other key ideas. • Not effective when careful, detailed reading is necessary.
HIGHLIGHTING PLUS MARKING		
After reading a section, *highlight words* or *phrases* representing key ideas. *Add markings* to summarize, organize, and/or emphasize important information.	• Beneficial if you need to know *much text information,* that is, main ideas *plus* details. • An effective *and* convenient method of *emphasizing ideas* right on the page.	• Effectiveness is greatly reduced if you highlight *too much* or *too little,* or if you don't add markings. • Can consume more time than other types of study guides.
OUTLINING		
Write key points in your own words; indent for progressive details. Add explanations or examples.	• Effective if you prefer to *rewrite information* for maximum recall. • Worthwhile if you prefer to learn material in a *linear format.*	• By just rewriting boldfaced headings and subheadings, you will create an easy, but *ineffective,* study guide.
STUDY CARDS		
On front, write question, term, concept, or main idea. *On back,* write definition, explanation, example, or supporting details.	• Especially effective for recall of *terms and definitions.* • Separates information into individual parts. • An easy format for oral quizzes.	• Tendency to *memorize,* as opposed to *learning,* new info. • Difficult to effectively show how ideas are related or organized.
VISUAL GUIDES—*maps, summary charts, timelines*		
A concise summary that indicates how ideas are organized or related. A variety of formats: idea map, summary chart, or timeline.	• Forms a *visual* picture of written material, which increases recall. • An *efficient* way to read: when you "fill in" the frame of the chart or map you created, you eliminate unneeded information.	• Can be difficult or confusing, especially if you are unused to identifying relationships among ideas. • Limits the amount of details that can be included.

CHAPTER 1	CHAPTER 2	CHAPTER 3	CHAPTER 4	CHAPTER 5	CHAPTER 6	CHAPTER 7	CHAPTER 8
Academic Success	Managing Time	Study Environment	Active Listening	Reading Textbooks	**Enhancing Memory**	Test Success	Continuing Success

CHAPTER 6

Enhancing Your Memory

FOCUS QUESTIONS

Describe the six memory-enhancing techniques presented in this chapter.

What is the connection between sleep, time management, and memory?

Describe a situation in which you used your senses to enhance your memory.

CHAPTER TERMS

After reading the chapter, define (in your own words) and provide an example for each of the following terms:

- association
- mnemonic device
- visualization

ESSENTIAL INGREDIENTS

College Studying

Memory:
The Essential Ingredients

Regrettably, a magical formula to boost one's memory does not exist. It is the commonsense study habits and strategies, implemented on a consistent basis, that strengthen memory. Many of these strategies have been described in Chapters 2–5. This chapter highlights six fundamental ingredients to enhance learning and improve memory. These are:

1. Get enough sleep.
2. Study in small, regular blocks of time.
3. Review soon after receiving new information.
4. Organize and categorize information.
5. Use your senses.
6. Associate ideas.

Get Enough Sleep

Regular, adequate nighttime sleep is a critical element of the memory process. College students between 18 and 21 years old function best with 8 to 10 hours of sleep per night. Research studies have demonstrated the drastic and negative effect that inadequate sleep has on a person's performance, concentration, and memory.

Although uninterrupted nighttime sleep plays a crucial role in recall, daytime naps also can benefit academic performance, as illustrated by Eve's experience:

> **A STUDENT'S VOICE**
>
> "Three or four days a week, I take what I refer to as a "power nap." A power nap is lying down and sleeping for an hour in the afternoon. If I sleep more than one hour, I wake up feeling tired, not refreshed. Since I work until 2:00 A.M. some mornings and never get the same amount of sleep every night, these power naps are important to me." —EVE

The bottom line is that a well-rested student understands and remembers more and therefore performs better than the sleep-deprived student.

Study in Small, Regular Blocks of Time

Your memory will be clearer at the *beginning* and at the *end* of any task or situation; it is the middle section that often becomes muddled and less clear. For instance, you likely remember the beginning stage of high school, when you were a new freshman going into an unfamiliar building, meeting new teachers, having new challenges, and so forth. In addition, the last part of your high school experiences—your senior year—likely provides memorable impressions in your mind. The middle years tend to be less distinct and more tangled.

Also consider the amount of time you schedule for study sessions. Most people lose their mental energy and concentration after 30 to 60 minutes, so plan accordingly. You can increase your mental recall by simply dividing one long study session into shorter sessions of no more than an hour. Take a short break between sessions by switching activities. This change of activities provides your brain with time to rest and to process the information that, in turn, strengthens your recollection. (*Note:* This strategy also applies when scheduling classes; you likely will learn and remember more in three one-hour class sessions per week as opposed to one three-hour class session.)

Therefore, a method of increasing your memory is to study information in *small blocks of time* with a *short break between sessions*. The blocks of study time that you set aside for an assignment depend on certain factors:

- **Subject matter.** Most students are able to concentrate for longer periods of time when working with material they find *interesting* or *relevant*.
- **Difficulty level.** Most students can concentrate longer when the information is *not so difficult* as to cause frustration, *nor so easy* as to cause boredom.
- **Time of day.** Students stay focused longer when they are feeling *fresh* and *alert*.

Plan ahead and consider the above factors when scheduling blocks of time for study and review.

Review Soon After Receiving New Information

Repetition embeds information in the mind and therefore is key to memory. Begin reviewing *soon* after your initial exposure to the information so that you don't have to "relearn" the subject matter.

"I found out that most people retain only about 20 percent of what they "learned" during the day. Therefore, rereading my class notes at night has been a good idea; it works as a reinforcement. I also review my textbook material more frequently. This has made test preparation go a lot easier and quicker for me. Plus there are fewer things on the test that do not look familiar." —BEN

Organize and Categorize Information

The more you can establish *relationships among* ideas, the more you tend to remember the ideas. *Linking* or *grouping* information will enhance your recall of the subject matter. For example, a student studying for an upcoming quiz in a biology class created the summary chart in Figure 6.1. Note the three distinct categories and four parallel phases under each category. This student created an organized framework by which to remember key information.

Use Your Senses

Review information regularly, using as many of your senses as possible, as discussed on the following pages.

FIGURE **6.1** *Example of organizing and categorizing.*

MITOSIS	MEIOSIS I	MEIOSIS II
Prophase:	Prophase I:	Prophase II:
Metaphase:	Metaphase I:	Metaphase II:
Anaphase:	Anaphase I:	Anaphase II:
Telophase:	Telophase I:	Telophase II:

Example of visualization.   FIGURE **6.2**

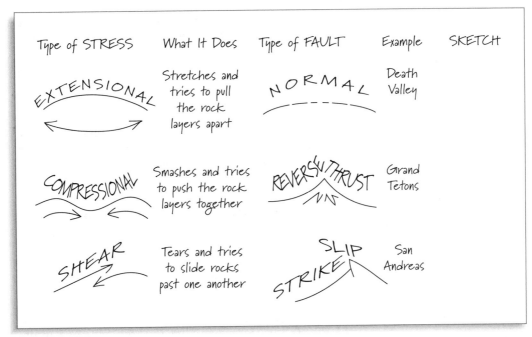

[created by Heather Kline]

• **Seeing.** Create visual pictures, and illustrate and color-code ideas. **Visualization,** forming a mental picture, is a vital component of memory. By visualizing information, you will be implanting images in your mind and thus retaining more. For instance, for a geoscience course, a student created an organized framework with several visual emphases; she added gradients and differences in lettering as well as a column to sketch each type of stress/fault (see Figure 6.2).

"I feel that if I write something out on paper, I am more likely to remember it than if I just underline or highlight it. For example, in choosing a textbook study guide, I prefer to write down important ideas in my notebook next to the class notes referring to the same topic. If needed, I will draw pictures or diagrams from the book into my notes. By integrating a text chapter with class notes, I am able to see the whole picture at once. Currently, I am enjoying the feeling of really *knowing* the material." —**NIKITA**

STUDENT VOICES

- **Saying.** Talk to yourself or to others. Join a study group in order to discuss and teach one another the subject matter.

- **Hearing.** Recite aloud in order to hear the information. Again, studying with others will provide opportunities to listen to people talking about the subject matter.

- **Touching.** Use your sense of touch to emphasize shapes, textures, and contours of materials. For example, for a geology course, try *feeling* different types of rocks or tracing the outlines of geological formations.

- **Doing.** *Write down* information, *act out* scenarios, *play* a game, or simply *move about* while reciting information. For example, students in a study group for a general psychology course played Charades when trying to remember psychological disorders. They acted out the various types of disorders while others guessed the name of the disorder and corresponding treatment. Reviewing information using a similar action game can make a profound and lasting impact on your memory.

pause.... *and reflect*

The first five ingredients for enhancing memory—(1) get adequate sleep; (2) study in small, regular blocks of time; (3) review soon after receiving new information; (4) organize and categorize; and (5) use your senses—were presented in previous chapters.

1. Refer to Chapter 2, "Managing Your Time," and reconsider the elements of sleep and regular blocks of study time.

- In order to improve your memory skills, where should you make changes?
- Do you need to increase sleep by going to bed earlier or adding power naps?

2. Refer to Chapter 4, "Active Listening and Note Taking," and reevaluate your habits.

- Should you add review time soon after certain classes to improve your learning?
- What do you do with your lecture notes to enhance your understanding and, ultimately, recall of important information?
- Do you need to create more or different study guides for lecture notes in order to improve your memory of key information?

3. Refer to the "Visual Study Guides: Maps, Summary Charts, and Timelines" section of Chapter 5, "Reading and Studying Textbooks," (page 86). Development of a visual study guide involves identifying and organizing key

ideas within a visual format; thus maps, summary charts, and timelines often enhance retention.

- How often do you create and use visual study guides when reading?
- How about when preparing for an exam? Have you developed a study guide that summarizes course material in a concise, visual format?
- Describe a map, chart, or timeline that was effective in improving your recall in a particular subject.

Associate Ideas

Association means relating or linking new information to that with which you are familiar. By connecting *new* ideas with *"old" ideas* already rooted in your mind, you can form memorable images to boost immediate recall. Be inventive and unique when linking ideas together; silly, exaggerated, or bizarre associations will produce lasting remembrances.

Association is best employed for *short-term* recall of facts and details that you tend to forget because the information is complex, unfamiliar, meaningless, or without context. For example, a student in a chemistry course created the following association to help her remember the details of the structure of the atom:

"Visualize an **atom** as an apartment *building:* an atom has many different **shells,** and an apartment building has many different *floors.* Each shell has **subshells,** and each floor holds *apartments* of differing sizes. The apartments are collections of *rooms,* and the subshells are collections of **orbitals.**"

—Carly M. Solazzo

pause... *and reflect*

Mnemonic Devices are another type of memory tool best used for short-term recall of details. An effective mnemonic device is simple to devise and easy to remember. The disadvantages of mnemonic devices include the following:

- You are *remembering*, not *learning*, information.
- They can be cumbersome to create and easily confused when you most want to remember details accurately and clearly, that is, when taking the test!

EXAMPLES OF MNEMONIC DEVICES

1. *Creating a catchy rhyme, jingle, or song*
   - Remembering specific biology researchers and the types of cells each studied:

     "People go slipping and **Schliden** on **Plant** cells and **Schwann** (swan) for **Animal** cells."

- Remembering the number of days in each month:

  "Thirty days has September, April, June, and November; all the rest have 31, except February, which has 28."

2. *Using the first letter of words to develop a phrase or acronym*
   - A campus building: *Hadley Union Building* = "HUB"
   - Piaget's Stages of Cognitive Development:

Shelia	(Sensorimotor)
and	
Peter	(Preoperational)
Counted	(Concrete Operational)
Frogs	(Formal Operational)

When have you used mnemonic devices to remember details? Describe several situations to share with classmates.

Conclusion

The grid in Figure 6.3 lists the memory techniques presented in this chapter. Summarize the techniques by completing the chart: add a description of the strategy, an example of how you've used it, and comments regarding its effectiveness. Add other strategies at the bottom.

Summary grid.

FIGURE   6.3

MEMORY STRATEGY	DESCRIPTION	EXAMPLE	COMMENTS
Adequate Sleep			
Small Blocks of Time			
Review Soon After			
Organize/ Categorize			
Use Your Senses			
Association			
Mnemonic Devices			
Other			

CHAPTER 7

Success with Tests

FOCUS QUESTIONS

What is the relationship between test-taking anxiety, test preparation, and test-taking performance?

Compare and contrast preparation for objective tests versus essay tests.

Describe three elements of test-wiseness that you will use this semester.

CHAPTER TERMS

After reading this chapter, define (in your own words) and provide an example for each of the following terms:

- deep muscle relaxation
- desensitization
- directive words
- mental imagery
- mental trigger
- performance anxiety
- qualifying words
- test anxiety
- test-wiseness

ESSENTIAL INGREDIENTS

College Studying

Success with Tests: Four Essential Ingredients

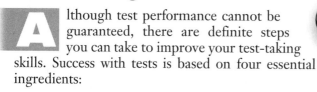

Although test performance cannot be guaranteed, there are definite steps you can take to improve your test-taking skills. Success with tests is based on four essential ingredients:

1. Be prepared.
2. Reduce your test anxiety.
3. Develop test-wiseness.
4. Review the test.

Be Prepared

KEEP UP WITH ACADEMIC WORK

Test preparation starts from the first day of the semester. Maintaining regular study *throughout each week* is a crucial element of test preparation. If you have followed strategies suggested in previous chapters, you likely are ready to study for (as opposed to cram for) the upcoming exam:

- Have you attended all classes and taken appropriate notes?
- Have you sought information about class sessions or assignments that you missed or were unsure about?
- Have you reviewed your notes soon after each class—clarifying, organizing, emphasizing, and summarizing key ideas?
- Have you kept pace with reading assignments—creating some type of study guide that represents important ideas?
- Have you reviewed weekly, either with a classmate, tutor, or study group, or by yourself?

If you answered "yes" to all or most of the above questions, you have been integrating study with day-to-day academic demands and thus are well prepared for the next step: *reviewing* and *consolidating* subject matter before the exam.

DEVELOP TEST REVIEW GUIDES

Plan for added study time each day during the week before a major test. During this added time, select, combine, and organize key information from class notes and readings and create concise review guides. Look for the major topics, often repeated in both readings and class notes; then dissect these major topics into related subtopics. Think about how the topics are connected. For example:

- Topic A is *part of* topic B.
- Topic A is *the opposite of* topic B.
- Topic A *results in* topic B.
- Topic B is *an example of* topic A.
- Topic B *describes* topic A.
- Topic B is *a function of* topic A.

Since test items often reflect these topics and connections, make sure they are part of your study guide, as illustrated in the following pages.

Study cards (Figure 7.1) are useful when you expect to have many terms or concepts on an upcoming test. On an index card, write the term or concept on the front and a summary, definition, explanation, or other associated ideas on the back. Study cards are effective for test review because they are handy and flexible; use them to review while waiting in line, between classes or appointments, in a bus or car, and so on.

Study cards to review for psychology test.   FIGURE **7.1**

OBSERVATION

Study behavior in natural setting.

<u>Adv</u>: normal setting

<u>Disadv</u>: no cause/effect

CASE STUDIES

Info. gathered about specific individuals.

<u>Adv</u>: detailed

<u>Disadv</u>: a lot of time

Maps and *charts* (Figure 7.2) are effective tools for test review because they help you to select, organize, and categorize important ideas and details in a visual format—key strategies for enhancing your recall of information.

REHEARSE FOR THE EXAM

Practice test questions. Prepare for an upcoming exam by answering questions similar to the type of questions that you expect to be on the test. By completing practice questions, you are reviewing the subject matter while familiarizing yourself to the format by which the information will be presented (that is, as essay, multiple choice, true/false, matching, identification,

FIGURE **7.2**   *Review chart for history test.*

VIETNAM: Progression of Events

Vietnam Events	WHAT is it?/WHY important?	WHO?	WHEN?
Domino Theory (escalation)	Like row of dominos—if one country falls, so will the rest.	Eisenhower	1954
Dien Bien Phu (escalation)	French troops parachute into a fort; terrible loss; only 200 of 1,400 escape.	French	1954
"Flexible Response" (escalation)	2,000 "advisors" going to Vietnam to research what is going on.	JFK	1960
Gulf of Tonkin (escalation)	Advises the president to take "all necessary measures."	LBJ	Aug. 1964
Tet Offensive (escalation)	Widens the scope of the war.		1968
"Peace with Honor" (withdrawal)	Nixon's election slogan—take U.S. troops out of Vietnam w/ honor.	Nixon	Nov. 1968
My Lai Massacre (withdrawal)	Public outrage w/ revelations that U.S. soldiers massacre 500 noncombative civilians.	U.S. soldiers; Charlie Team; William Calley	March 1968 breaks in Dec.
The Pentagon Papers (withdrawal)	Reveals everything about the war.	Daniel Ellsberg	June 1971

[created by Melissa Swope]

and/or sentence completion questions). Use the end-of-chapter or separate study guide questions, or create your own practice questions. If you participate in a study group, ask each person to make up practice questions to share with the others.

"I am an English major; thus keeping up with the reading is of utmost importance. Most importantly, I try to attend all of my classes because a large part of the test questions seem to come straight from class sessions. The week before the test, I usually have the bulk of all material read, which leaves the last several days for review, reinforcement, and mini-quizzes. Lately, I have been feeling more confident about my learning, and my test scores reflect this." —KESHIA

STUDENT VOICES

Teach others. An additional type of rehearsal is to run through the material by "teaching" the information to another person. When you are able to clearly explain information to others, you likely know it. Convince a roommate, family member, or friend to be the designated "student," or teach the material to yourself. In the role of "teacher," you will be training yourself to thoroughly know the information. At the very least, saying the information out loud will help reinforce what you *do* and *do not* know.

"First, I allow myself four to five days to study for a test. Second, I anticipate what questions may be on a test and then find a family member to 'teach' the subject matter to. By using these three strategies I have already increased my grade in two classes." —SAM

STUDENT VOICES

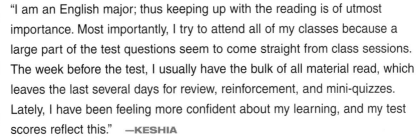

try it out!

1. Identify a *subject* in which you will be having a major exam in the near future:
2. In *preparation* for the exam, answer the following questions:
   • When is the exam?

- What topics and material are to be covered in the exam?
- What type of questions will be on the exam?
- Have you been keeping up with course work for this subject? If not, where have you been falling behind and what do you still need to do?

3. Continue preparing for the exam by creating a *test review guide*—either study cards or a map or chart.

4. Next, develop a *practice exam*, using questions similar to the type you expect to be on the real exam.

5. Continue *rehearsing* for the exam by teaching key concepts to another person.

6. *After* you have taken the exam, **Assess Your Success** with the methods of preparation that you used for this test.

- Which preparation strategies did you find to be especially effective and why?
- Which strategies were *not* effective for you? Why?
- How will you approach preparing for the next exam in this subject?

Reduce Test Anxiety

DO YOU HAVE TEST ANXIETY?

Preparation is a key factor in reducing extreme worry and anxiousness associated with taking a test. However, at times, even the best-prepared student gets trapped in a cycle of excessive anxiety. **Test anxiety,** a type of **performance anxiety,** is based on the apprehensive thoughts and emotional feelings associated with how well you will do on an exam.

Consider this example: Two people look outside and see bright sunlight. One person thinks, "Great weather! I can't wait to go swimming today!" Another person sees the *same* bright sunlight but thinks, "Darn it—I'm disappointed that I have to water the grass and flowers again today." These two people have completely *different thoughts*—and subsequent *feelings*—about the *same situation.*

Similarly, people have differences in thoughts and feelings in regard to test taking. One student might think of an exam as a personal challenge, whereas another thinks of the same exam as a personal threat. It is the latter student who worries, often excessively, about the test and, as a consequence, often exhibits symptoms of anxiety.

your THOUGHTS [worry]

↓ lead to ↓

your FEELINGS [anxiety]

Test-taking anxiety is a condition that *interferes with positive test results.* How anxious are you when taking a test? Would you have performed better *if* you weren't so uneasy and fearful? The following assessment can provide an estimate of your level of test anxiety.

try it out!

Test Anxiety Assessment

Complete by checking *Yes, Sometimes,* or *No* for each of the twelve statements:

WHEN PREPARING FOR OR TAKING A TEST:	YES	SOMETIMES	NO
1. I think about whether I'm going to pass or fail.	○	○	○
2. I keep wishing the exam was over.	○	○	○
3. I worry that I am not doing well.	○	○	○
4. I can't stop thinking about how nervous I feel.	○	○	○
5. My stomach gets upset.	○	○	○
6. My heart beats very fast.	○	○	○
7. I often freeze up, and my mind goes blank.	○	○	○
8. I feel hot and sweaty.	○	○	○
9. I feel very tense.	○	○	○
10. I forget information that I really know.	○	○	○
11. I often get panicky.	○	○	○
12. I tend to breathe faster.	○	○	○

SCORING – Total your points using the following key:

Each *Yes* = 2 points
Each *Sometimes* = 1 point
Each *No* = 0 points
Your total points = _____

(You'll have a total score between 0 and 24.)

The *higher* your total score on the Test Anxiety Assessment, the more *anxious* you are when taking a test. If your score is between 10 and 24, you'll likely benefit from working on strategies to reduce the worry and anxiety associated with test taking.

Note that items 1–4 on the assessment refer to those thoughts that negatively affect your test-taking performance. Worry over such things as your test results, whether you are going to pass the course, whether you will make it through college, or even your parents' reactions can interfere with test performance. Excessive worry can lead to a physical reaction toward test taking, including sweaty palms, rapid breathing, dizziness, and so on. Assessment items 5–12 refer to this *physical response*. Thus, apprehension plus a physiological response results in full-blown test anxiety.

Keep in mind that not all worry and anxiety is bad. In fact, *some* anxiousness can be good in that it keeps your adrenaline flowing and, as a result, gives you that edge to perform better. However, you do not want your anxiety to be excessive to the point that it interferes with your performance. If you think that you *could have done better* on a test if you weren't so anxious, then you need to tackle ways to reduce this anxiety.

pause.... *and reflect*

Refer back to your total score on the Test Anxiety Assessment.

- If your total score is *less than 10:* reflect about why your anxiety is low. Consider how you approach a test—that is, how you *think* about exams and what you *do* that keeps anxiety at a minimum? Why don't you worry excessively?

- If your total score is *10 or above:* think about those *situations* that trigger worry and anxiety for you. Some circumstances that set off anxiousness might be

  - The word "test" on the syllabus or board.
  - The night before the exam.
  - The morning of the exam.
  - Walking into the classroom to take the exam.
  - Hearing other students talk about the exam.
  - The instructor passing out the exam to the class.
  - A test item that you're not sure how to answer.
  - Waiting to get back the results.

Come up with *at least three or four scenarios* that apply to you. Beside each scenario, write the *exact thoughts* that run through your mind when you are in that situation. For example, for the situation: "A test item that you're not sure how to answer," you might have these thoughts: "Oh no, I'm going to fail!" or "I should know this answer," or "This is terrible!"

CHANGE HOW YOU THINK ABOUT THE TEST

Since your thoughts lead to your feelings, one way to diminish feelings of test anxiety is to change your thoughts about tests.

Focus on the *present*, not the past or the future. Test-anxious students tend to focus their thoughts on what occurred previously ("I did poorly on the last quiz") or what they predict to occur ("I'm going to fail this test"). Bear in mind that your past performance does *not* foretell your present performance. Likewise, you cannot accurately predict what the outcome of a test will be. Therefore, keep your thoughts focused on the here and now, that is, your present place in time. Be alert to the thoughts that run through your head; if you begin to think about past or future events, *stop* and redirect your thoughts to what you are doing or can do *now*. Deter yourself from thinking about an imaginary future and, instead, think about the realistic present moment in time. For example:

"I did poorly on the last chemistry quiz and am going to fail this upcoming quiz."

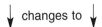 changes to

"I am doing practice problems in anticipation of the next chemistry quiz."

Put the test in perspective. Test-anxious students tend to overinflate the importance of any single test. In the realm of worldly events, any one exam is not *that* important! Keep a realistic, less extreme perspective about quizzes and tests. Students sometimes are helped by playing out, in their minds, a frightening chain of events linked to test performance. This tactic produces scenarios that often are exaggerated and ridiculous. As an example, the following is the chain of thoughts for one anxious student:

"I am going to fail this biology test."

which leads to

"I am going to flunk the biology course."

which leads to

"I am going to be on academic probation."

which leads to

"I am going to flunk out of college."

which leads to

"I am going to be flipping hamburgers for the rest of my life!"

Hopefully this student realizes that it is neither logical nor realistic to think that failing a biology test will result in a lifetime of flipping hamburgers. Being aware of unreasonable thinking patterns can help you maintain a more balanced view of a test.

Recognize your choices. "I *have to* do well" or "I *must* get an 'A'" are common thoughts of students fretting over a test. These thoughts imply that the student has no other options *but* to perform well—or even perfectly! Practice eliminating the phrases "have to," "required to," "should," and "must" from your thoughts. Instead, replace them with phrases that suggest you have options, such as "I *prefer to* do well" or "I'd *rather* improve my score on the next exam." Mindfully choose words that evoke personal choices and the leeway and sense of freedom that come with these choices.

Be positive. Be alert to your negative, and even apathetic, thoughts. Instead, focus on positive, encouraging aspects of yourself and your actions. Choose words that reflect optimism and personal affirmation. Also, seek encouragement from family and friends. As a result, you will feel more upbeat and confident about taking tests. For example:

"I'm so angry at myself for getting a 'C' on this quiz!"

 is replaced with

"It's *okay* that I received a 'C'; I'll probably *improve* on the next quiz."

"I don't care what I do on this test!"

 is replaced with

"I will try to earn a reasonable grade on this test."

pause... *and reflect*

Do you see yourself reflected in any of these thought patterns? Refer back to page 118 where you identified specific thoughts associated with testing situations. Using the previous suggestions for changing how you think about a test, create *new* statements to reflect a change in your own thought pattern.

CHANGE HOW YOU PHYSICALLY REACT TO A TEST

Because test-anxious students view the exam as threatening, their bodies react as in any other intimidating or frightening situation: breathing becomes more shallow and rapid, the heart beats faster, muscles tense, adrenaline flows throughout the body, skin becomes sweaty, and digestion slows down. This physical reaction is appropriate when a situation is actually threatening, such as spotting an animal running in front of your car when you are driving. In that situation, it *is* appropriate that your body becomes tense as you focus only on not hitting the animal. However, these same intense physical symptoms work *against* you when taking a test; tense muscles, rapid breathing, upset stomach, and so forth can cause you to lose your concentration and mental acuity. Instead of focusing on the content of the exam, you become focused on your extreme and even frightening physical reactions. However, by using two simple techniques, **mental imagery** and **deep muscle relaxation,** you can greatly alter your physical response to a test.

"Since I'm usually well prepared for exams, you'd think that I'd be more relaxed come exam time. I just can't seem to walk into a room knowing I'm going to take a test, and be calm. Deep breathing does help—some. I take a couple of breaths before I walk into the test room (at least I know I'm still breathing, right?). I think I'm hopeless, so the thing I do is talk to myself, which I've become a pro at. I just try to put each test into perspective. I point out that I am prepared, I've studied, and that one test won't blow my grade. This helps to bring me from 'high-strung' to just plain 'nervous,' but this isn't all bad. I think it's the perfectionist's advantage—being able to handle a nervous, pressure situation." **—RACHEL**

STUDENT VOICES

Mental imagery. Your mind plays a powerful role in determining your physical response to an event. A calm, peaceful image in your mind can result in a tranquil, stress-free physical response. Think of an event in your own past that evokes a feeling of personal contentment, joy, or satisfaction. Use all of your senses to reconstruct a realistic version of this event. Imagine yourself in that situation: What are you specifically doing? What sounds do you hear? What are you saying? Can you smell or taste anything? What are you feeling? Because this situation activates a feeling of calm and contentment within you, it is called your **mental trigger.** Use this mental trigger often. Become accustomed to generating this mental image to prompt a response of easy relaxation.

Deep breathing and muscle relaxation. You likely tense your muscles when a stressful, threatening situation arises. This tense, rigid bodily response can rapidly lead to feelings of panic, which result in poor test performance. With directed practice, you can train yourself how to replace the tense response with a calming response.

One type of deep muscle relaxation exercises begins with monitoring your breathing by being mindful of slow, full, even breaths that originate deep in your abdomen (as opposed to shallow breaths originating in your upper chest).

Do this exercise when you have a chunk of time by yourself, in a darkened, quiet room, with your eyes closed. Next, focus on relaxing your muscles from the top of your head down through the trunk of your body and your limbs to your toes. Concentrate on one group of muscles at a time, letting those muscles become loose and relaxed. Picture your muscles becoming heavy, like a wet mop. By loosening your muscles, you will be calming your body. With practice over time, you will be able to easily and quickly create this feeling of deep relaxation and, as a result, free your mind to concentrate on such tasks as preparing for or taking an exam.

DESENSITIZE YOURSELF

Desensitization refers to a gradual yet steady exposure to the anxiety-producing event. Desensitization begins by breaking down the event—in this case, test taking—into small and specific anxiety-producing situations. You place the situations in order: from *least* to *most* anxiety producing. Starting with the situation creating the least anxiety, you combine mental imagery (imagining oneself in the particular situation) with deep muscle relaxation techniques. Monitor your physical responses while you practice mentally "being" in the specific situation. Build toward "real" exposure to the test-taking situation; continue to monitor both your mental and your physical reactions.

"Taking a test used to be one of my worst nightmares; I had almost every symptom of test anxiety. I used to get so mad for allowing myself to get so upset. I created so much pressure for myself, including whether I would pass or fail, how low my GPA was, that the instructor hated me, how dumb I felt, I should have studied more, etc.—all of which affected the way I took a test. I was so relieved to find ways to overcome the fear of a test.

"The first improvement I made was to complete my studying on a daily basis, instead of cramming during an all-night study binge. By covering the material on a regular basis, I don't feel the need to cram and my anxiety has greatly diminished. I begin preparing for a test by reviewing my notes several days in advance. Now, when reviewing, I am able to readily recall important ideas, which makes studying less of a problem. If I do begin to feel tense, I relax myself by taking deep breaths. To counter my fear of professors, I ask questions either after class or during office hours. This permits me to feel more comfortable with taking a test." **—SHANA**

As an example, one student identified the following scenarios as producing varying levels of personal anxiety:

"I have some anxiousness when I hear the instructor announce the date of the test. I then worry every time I see the word *test* in my planner. My anxiety really increases a few days before the test when I begin to study more. I have trouble sleeping the night before a major test. The peak of my anxiety is when I enter the classroom the day of the test!"

This student's anxiety builds for each succeeding scenario. For desensitization, the student begins with the *least anxiety-producing scenario:* "the instructor announces the date of the test." While in a state of deep muscle relaxation, the student creates a mental image of being in a specific classroom and hearing the instructor announce a test date. The student rehearses thought patterns that counter anxiety, such as "I'll prepare for this test the best that I can." The student repeats this image and related thoughts until he notices that his response is continually calm. At this point, he continues with desensitization by imagining the *next higher scenario:* "seeing the word *test* in my planner." He continues until his calm, relaxed responses readily translate to real-life test scenarios.

pause.... *and reflect*

1. Refer to Figure 7.3. In the left-hand, place a "✓" in the circle beside each of the listed situations that result in *some level* of worry or anxiety for you.
2. Order the circles with "✓'s," from *least* anxiety producing (write a 1 on the line next to that circle) to *most* anxiety producing.
3. To the right of each item with a ✓, write *at least one way* that you can reduce anxiety by changing your *thoughts*, your *actions*, and/or your *preparation techniques*.

try it out!

1. Use **mental imagery:** In your mind, identify and recreate a scene that triggers a sense of calmness.
2. Combine your mental image with **deep muscle relaxation.** Practice breathing and systematically relaxing all of your muscles. Do this exercise at least twice a day for 15- to 30-minute sessions when you are able to turn off lights, be comfortable, and not be disturbed by others.

FIGURE **7.3**   *Reducing test anxiety.*

Causes of Test Worry and Anxiety	Ways to Reduce or Eliminate
◯ ____ The first test of the semester.	
◯ ____ The test counts toward a big chunk of the final grade.	
◯ ____ The test covers lots of material.	
◯ ____ I don't fully understand the material.	
◯ ____ I don't feel prepared for the test.	
◯ ____ I don't feel competent with the type of questions.	
◯ ____ I allowed too little time for studying for the test.	
◯ ____ I am taking more than one test during the day.	
◯ ____ I've previously performed poorly in the course.	
◯ ____ I'm afraid that I'm going to forget key information.	
◯ ____ I feel pressure to get a good grade in the course.	
◯ ____ I'm thinking about my parents' or instructor's expectations.	
◯ ____ I'm concerned about my overall GPA.	
◯ ____ I'm afraid of failing.	
◯ ____ I'm concerned about my future job prospects.	
◯ ____ Any other?	

3. Practice **desensitization.** Begin with the *least anxiety producing* situation that you previously identified.

4. **Assess Your Success** by answering the following questions:

- How have you progressed with the above process? Explain your progress with each step.
- After completing a test or quiz, have you noticed a reduction in your worry and anxiety? Describe the test-taking situation and your reaction.
- What will you continue to do to decrease your anxiety?

Develop Test-Wiseness

Test-wiseness refers to the skills and strategies related to *how to take* tests. It involves becoming familiar with and savvy about answering various types of questions: *objective* (true/false, multiple choice, matching, sentence completion) and *essay.* When used in combination with (not as a substitute for) thorough, sound preparation, test-wiseness can noticeably improve your test-taking performance.

USE A FOUR-STEP COURSE OF ACTION

Step 1. Before looking at the test itself, use the back of the paper or the margins to jot down details that are "crammed" into your head and that you are afraid of forgetting. This step will (1) unburden your mind of those nagging details, and (2) provide you with a means to focus your attention immediately and involve yourself in the test-taking process.

Step 2. Prior to answering any questions, quickly look over the entire test and note the

- Length of the test.
- Types of questions and point value attached to each type.
- General difficulty level.

"First, I skim through the test to see what it is like. By doing this step, I sometimes notice clues that help me figure out questions. Then, I complete all the questions that I know. This helps to calm me down and boosts my confidence." **—NOAH**

STUDENT VOICES

Also, *carefully* read the test instructions. Based on this information, strategize about how to approach the test given your time constraints. Generally, start with questions you can answer more readily or that are worth more points; then tackle the difficult, time-consuming items.

pause... *and reflect*

"Begin with objective questions, and then answer any essay questions."

Why is this strategy generally recommended for test taking? Do you agree with this suggestion? Why or why not?

Step 3. After completing questions you are sure of, go back and answer those questions that you left blank or put a question mark beside. At this point, you will be calmer and your mind will be clearer, allowing you to concentrate on how to answer the more difficult questions. Furthermore, now you might see clues to help you answer the questions you initially left blank.

Step 4. When you complete all items, go back and check for mistakes. Reread the test directions; you might discover that, in your haste, you misread directions the first time. Then, slowly reread each question. Use your *mouth*, though not your voice, to read and silently "hear" each question and answer. This technique will help you to vigilantly check for oversights and errors.

WATCH FOR KEY WORDS

Pay attention to word choices in test questions. Look for key words or phrases in both objective and essay questions that pinpoint requirements for a correct answer. As an example, examine the following multiple-choice test question:

"What is the main effect of the Hitler Jugend on events leading to the Holocaust?"

"Main effect" is the first key phrase; it implies that, although there may be many effects, your instructor is looking for the *main* or foremost effect. In addition, the word *effect* indicates that you are searching for a *cause and effect connection* between ideas. In other words, when answering this question, consider how "__ results in __."

Other key words are the *terms* associated with the subject or topic. For this question, "Hitler Jugend" and "Holocaust" are the crucial terms that complete the cause and effect connection and, thus, are central to the correct answer.

pause... *and reflect*

For the following test questions, identify the *key words*. Note *why* each key word is important for providing the correct answer.

1. "What was the Final Solution, and who proposed it?"
2. "Number the events in the order in which they occurred."
3. "List three similarities and three differences between WWI and WWII."
4. "What statement best describes the long-term effects of the post-WWII tension between the United States and Russia?"
5. "Choose three statements that accurately describe how married life and family income was affected by the influx of women into the workforce after WWII."

LOOK FOR QUALIFYING WORDS

Qualifying words are words or phrases that moderate an "extreme" idea in a statement. They indicate that the statement's message is *not* a hard-and-fast rule. The presence of qualifying words suggests that exceptions, omissions, misstatements, or errors are possible. Consider a continuum (Figure 7.4) with "absolute" and "extreme" words at either end: *absolutely* "yes" at one end and *absolutely* "no" at the other. In between the ends is the vast majority of qualifying words indicating moderation, possible oversights, special conditions, and so on.

Some messages *do* belong to one "extreme" or the other: "The earth *always* rotates on its axis" or "A human being *certainly* is not a reptile." Both of these statements contain extreme words and both happen to be *true* statements. However, *most* events fall somewhere *in between* the extreme ends:

- "It *definitely* rains in June." = FALSE
- "It *never* rains in June." = FALSE

Qualifying words.   FIGURE **7.4**

definitely absolutely	usually	somewhat	maybe	sometimes	perhaps	in my judgment	never have to
YES		IN-BETWEEN 'QUALIFYING WORDS'					**NO**
always certainly	most	typically	possibly	generally	to some extent	in my opinion	none

- "It *usually* rains in June." = TRUE (This statement allows for the one June 50 years ago in which we had absolutely no rain.)

Many (not *all*) statements containing qualifying words happen to be *true* statements. Therefore, if you are not sure of the correct answer when reading a true/false statement on a test, use these tips:

- If *qualifying words* are present, the statement *tends to be* true.
- If *absolute, extreme words* are present, the statement *often is* false.

Remember: This method does *not* replace studying and knowing subject matter. Consider this as a guide to assist you when you are stuck, *not* as a hard-and-fast rule.

try it out!

Mark the following statements as either "true" or "false." Why did you answer each item as you did? What **qualifying words** can you identify?

_____ 1. In the year 2150, the projected worldwide life expectancy will be 86 years old.

_____ 2. The world's crude-oil reserves likely will run out by the year 2063.

_____ 3. The belief that smoking threatens a person's health is not linked to that person's beliefs about the severity of cancer.

_____ 4. You should plan for some leisure activity during the day—everybody needs a break.

_____ 5. Stress plays a role in all physical illness because of its effect on the immune system.

PRACTICE MULTIPLE-CHOICE QUESTIONS

Multiple-choice questions are the most popular type of test question, particularly in large introductory-level courses. Think of multiple-choice questions as a series of true/false statements: the lead-in clause or statement is combined with each option, forming a series of longer statements that are either true or false. Your task, as the test taker, is to choose the *best* true option. A sample question follows:

1. In a test question, "compare" refers to:
   A. Differences among items.
   B. A relationship among items.

C. Similarities among items.

D. "A" + "B"

E. None of the above.

F. All of the above.

By combining the lead-in clause with each of the six options, there are essentially six "true/false" statements for this one question:

A. In a test question, "compare" refers to a list of items.

B. In a test question, "compare" refers to a relationship among items.

C. In a test question, "compare" refers to similarities among items.

D. In a test question, "compare" refers to a lsit of items and a relationship among items.

E. . . . and so on.

Note that options A–C are central to the answer since the remaining three options (D–F) are various combinations of the first three choices. Thus, you should focus on the first three statements (A–C) and identify each as being TRUE *or* FALSE:

A. In a test question, "compare" refers to a list of items.
   [*This statement is false.*]

B. In a test question, "compare" refers to a relationship among items.
   [*This statement is true since a relationship or connection does exist in a comparison.*]

C. In a test question, "compare" refers to similarities among items.
   [*This statement is definitely true since "compare" means "like" or "similar to."*]

You are searching for the *one* true statement as the answer. Given that you identified *two* true statements, look at the remaining three choices to see if "B + C" is an option. Only "A + B" is presented, and you can eliminate this option (D) since it is a *false* statement. Likewise, both options E and F have to be *false* (since *at least one* but *not all* of statements A–C are *true*). Thus, choose option C as your *best answer.*

In summary, viewing multiple-choice items as a series of true/false statements can simplify your test-taking approach, *especially* when multiple combinations are presented as options. As you read the lead-in clause with each option, write "T" or "F" beside that option, with the goal of ultimately choosing the one "T." If you have more than one "T," then look at the combinations, ultimately choosing the *best* option as your answer.

Strategies for choosing which option is *best* and which options can be *eliminated* are summarized next. If you are not sure of the "best" answer on a test, these strategies will help you to make *informed guesses.* In general:

1. Select the more *specific* and *inclusive* choice (this often is the *longest* option). Eliminate extremely general options.

2. Eliminate *grammatical mismatches* when combining the lead-in clause with an option, such as a plural subject with a singular verb.

3. Select an option that is *similar in format to others,* such as containing repeated terms, a similar structure, or the same word pattern.

4. If a *word or phrase is repeated* throughout the test, it tends to be part of a TRUE option at some point.

5. Focus on *familiar terminology* as possible true options. Instructors sometimes use vocabulary that does not relate to the subject matter; if you have never seen the term before, consider it as a false option.

6. When *"not"* is part of the lead-in clause, eliminate "not" when reading the statement and then search for the false option.

7. Be aware of *qualifying words* (which tend to be true) and *absolute words* (which tend to be false) in statements.

8. If you are not sure, use your *background knowledge, experiences,* and *common sense!*

9. If you are *not* being penalized for wrong answers, then don't leave an answer blank—you might as well *guess!*

10. A *middle option* tends to be correct more times than do beginning or ending options, especially when presented with a range of numbers.

11. "All of the above" is more often true; "none of the above" is more often false. Instructors prefer testing students about what is *present* on paper ("all of the above"), as opposed to what is *missing* ("none of the above").

try it out!

What is the *best* answer for each of the following multiple-choice questions? Write your reasons for selecting or eliminating options, using the previous list of strategies.

1. "Soy isolate" is:
    A. A white powdered food that is 90 percent protein.
    B. A white powdered food that is 90 percent carbohydrate.
    C. A chemical compound used in kitchen utensils.
    D. A + B.

2. The characteristics of "microtubules" include:
    A. They have a shape of straight, hollow tubes.
    B. They have a shape of solid rods.
    C. They have a size of approximately 25 nm.
    D. A + B.

E. A + C.

F. All of the above.

3. Which operations are associated with the information-processing model of memory?

A. Input, storage, and retrieval.

B. Input, rehearsal, and output.

C. Process, storage, and recall.

D. Encode, consolidate, and retrieval.

4. In one research study, college students had more accurate memories:

A. The students needed repetitive coaxing.

B. The students did not have more accurate memories.

C. When they exhibited abnormal disorders.

D. When they had high blood sugar levels.

5. An instructional method that does *not* enhance creative thought is:

A. Establishing preset rules.

B. Establishing collaborative learning groups.

C. Using illustrations.

PRACTICE ESSAY QUESTIONS

Expect to encounter essay questions, especially in social science courses and in smaller, higher-level courses. Instructors often expect students to exhibit higher-level thought processes when answering essay questions.

Have a clear understanding of **directive words**—those specific words in essay questions signaling *what the instructor expects in your answer.* Directive words orient you as to *what to include in* and *how to organize* your answer. Test your knowledge of directive words by completing the second column in Figure 7.5. (The first item is done for you.)

The following steps provide a general guideline to help you successfully complete essay-type test items.

Step 1. Be clear on the *type* and *length* of answer that your instructor expects.

- For a short-answer essay question, expect to write one to two paragraphs for your answer.

- For a longer essay question, write several substantial paragraphs, amounting to one or more pages in length.

FIGURE **7.5** *Directive words.*

Directive Words	What I Should Include in My Answer
Compare	***similarities*** between/among ideas; how "things" are **alike** (can also include differences)
Contrast	
Define	
Critique	
Describe	
Discuss	
Explain	
Evaluate	
Identify	
Illustrate	
Justify	
List	
Relate	
Summarize	
Trace	

Step 2. Read the question and *jot down your immediate thoughts*. What terms and ideas do you associate with the question?

Step 3. Circle or underline *key words* within the question, including:

- *Directive words*, such as those in Figure 7.5.
- Words or terms *linked* to the topic.

Step 4. Reflect on the *ideas* that will adequately answer the question, writing a draft as you move along.

- Decide about the *main* idea of your answer; then draft a *thesis statement* representing this main idea. Use key words in the question to form your introductory statement.

- Decide about appropriate *supporting ideas* and how to *organize* these ideas. What information will you include that *explains, supports,* or *relates* to your thesis?

- Decide about *specific evidence* or *examples* that make your answer more accurate and precise.

- Refer back to your immediate jottings (Step 2). Should you add any of these initial thoughts to your draft?

Step 5. Carefully read through your draft, mouthing the words so you will see and "hear" your ideas.

- Does your answer *make sense?* Are you answering *completely?*

- Are you *accurate* yet *concise?* (Do not pad your answer with excessive details—consider the impression your answer will make on your instructor, who will be reading a stack of similar answers!)

- Do your ideas *flow smoothly*—that is, are you *connecting thoughts* to increase the fluency of ideas?

Step 6. Read your answer *backward* so that you concentrate on each word and catch any spelling errors.

Figure 7.6 shows a question, a breakdown of the six-step process, and a sample answer.

try it out!

As practice, write a short essay answer for each focus question at the beginning of this chapter. Then, critique your answer using the following criteria.

○ Do you have a clearly written *thesis statement* that begins your answer? Establish your main idea at the start of your essay. This will focus your thoughts as the writer and your instructor's thoughts as the reader. When grading the tests, your instructor will be looking for key ideas in each of many essay exams. Therefore, make sure your key ideas are clearly stated at the start of your essay.

○ Have you provided *supporting ideas* for your thesis statement? Include adequate and accurate details (examples, evidence, characteristics, explanations) to strengthen your ideas.

○ Are your ideas *organized?*

○ Have you made appropriate *transitions* between ideas?

(continued on p. 136)

FIGURE **7.6**   *Sample essay question and answer.*

Sample Question

"Compare and contrast the leadership of Franklin D. Roosevelt and Adolf Hitler."

Step 1: The instructor expects some detail and/or examples to explain the main idea; length is approximately two to three paragraphs, 250–300 words.

Step 2: Immediate thoughts that the student associated with the question:

FDR—U. S. President; well liked, especially by lower class; New Deal to reverse Depression and poverty; optimistic; bad economic times.

Hitler—Germany; dictator; pessimistic; used Jews and others as scapegoats; bad economic times; well liked.

Step 3: Identify key words in the question.

"*Compare* and *contrast* the leadership of Franklin D. *Roosevelt* and Adolf *Hitler.*"

Step 4: (A) Create a thesis statement:

Roosevelt and Hitler were important world leaders but had different backgrounds and actions.

(B) Identify supporting ideas with specifics in chronological order:

- FDR born wealthy; Hitler born to civil servants.
- Both school dropouts.
- American and German people's resentment—Hoover administration (U. S.) and Weimar Republic (Germany).
- Initially, both not considered capable of leading.
- Democracy vs. dictatorship.
- Both had psychological influence on the public, emphasizing the current economic hardships and gaining popularity/support from the lower class.
- Roosevelt sympathized with the poor; he was honest about the present economic hardships but optimistic about the future—hope and confidence.
- Hitler emphasized hatred and violence against Jews, communists, the wealthy, and minorities, focusing on fears and projecting images of strength, power, and hard work.
- Both used radio for propaganda: Roosevelt—weekly "Fire Side Chat" for intimate connections with people. Hitler mandated radios; broadcast explosive speeches in front of cheering crowds.

Continued.   FIGURE **7.6**

(C) Identify connecting thoughts for "compare" and "contrast": similar; opposing; although; both; on the other hand; whereas; in contrast; different from; and; furthermore

After doing **Step 5** (carefully reading through the draft and revising) and **Step 6** (reading backward to catch spelling errors), the student completed the answer:

Completed Answer

Franklin Roosevelt and Adolf Hitler were significant world leaders who had both similar and opposing backgrounds, personality characteristics, and leadership styles. Roosevelt was born to a wealthy and influential political family of New York. On the other hand, Hitler was a child of a minor civil servant in Austria; he adopted Germany as his homeland later on. Both shared experiences as school dropouts and spent some perplexing years before they found their niche in politics.

Their rise to power in the 1933 elections was a result of resentment by the American and German people—resentment against the Hoover administration in the United States and against the Weimar Republic in Germany. Initially, both leaders were not considered to be capable of their new positions. Under Hitler, a one-party dictatorship was established, whereas Roosevelt led a democratic government in the United States.

Both Hitler and Roosevelt had great psychological influence on the public. Both emphasized the current economic hardships, gaining popularity and support from the lower class of their countries. Roosevelt sympathized with the poor; he was honest about the present economic hardships but optimistic about the future. He infused the American people with hope and confidence. In contrast, Hitler's popularity was built on a platform of hatred and violence against Jews, communists, the wealthy, and other minorities. He focused on people's fears, projecting images of strength, power, and hard work to counter those fears.

Furthermore, both leaders masterfully used the radio for broadcasting propaganda. Roosevelt hosted a weekly "Fireside Chat" in order to make intimate connections with the American people. Hitler mandated that all households in Germany have radios. Different from Roosevelt in style, only Hitler's explosive speeches in front of cheering crowds were broadcast to the German people.

In summary, Franklin Roosevelt and Adolf Hitler were influential world leaders who, though outwardly different, shared a number of leadership traits.

[Contributed by Yue Ying Zhang]

○ Include such words as *also, in addition, for example, such as, on the other hand, first, second, then, next, therefore, as a result,* and *in summary.*

○ Have you included a simple, tightly worded *conclusion?* End with a simple rewording of the thesis.

○ Is your answer clearly written without padding extra words or ideas?

○ Is the essay easy to read and understand?

○ Is your essay free of all spelling and grammar errors?

Remember: your instructor will be reading many answers to the same question. Therefore, strive to create an answer that correctly and distinctively illustrates your understanding of the subject matter.

Review the Test

The often-heard adage is true—you *do* learn from your mistakes! Receiving a test score is not enough; go back over test items, especially those that you answered incorrectly, in an effort to improve your performance on the next test for that course. If your instructor does not pass back the exam or does not use class time to review common errors, make an appointment to review your test during the instructor's office hours. Sometimes instructors allow students to go over test material with a graduate teaching assistant, a trusted tutor, or a faculty member specializing in learning skills.

When reviewing your test, study how the test items are constructed. Most test items require more than pure memorization. Instead, you are required to relate ideas, apply concepts, distinguish similarities or differences, identify effects, or examine case studies. Taking the time and effort to carefully review a previous test is a valuable strategy in preparing you for the next test. As you continue to take class notes, read, and do assignments for a course, think ahead to the next exam: What will you need to know, and how will the information be presented on the test?

In addition, when reviewing a test, pay special attention to your errors. Generally, mistakes are due to one or more of the following causes:

• **Insufficient preparation**—not understanding and remembering the content well enough.

• **Inadequate test-taking skills**—not knowing how to approach the particular types of questions on the test.

• **Extreme anxiety**—which interferes with your test performance.

As you examine what you did right and wrong on the test, consider (1) what you can do to better prepare yourself for the next test, and (2) where you can go or who you can see for added support and guidance (your instructor, a study group, or a Learning Center, Tutorial Center, or Counseling Center).

pause... *and reflect*

Identify a recent test that you will review, either in class or out of class. Spend time carefully examining your responses. Do you recognize patterns of how you tend to approach and answer questions? *Why* did you make errors on this test (insufficient preparation, inadequate test-taking skills, or extreme anxiety)? *How* will you prepare for your next test?

try it out!

Learning Style and Test Taking

The following steps will help you decide how you best prepare for and take an exam.

1. Write your four-letter "type" (as identified in Chapter 1):
   - **E** Extraversion   or   **I** Introversion,
   - **S** Sensing   or   **N** Intuition,
   - **T** Thinking   or   **F** Feeling, and
   - **J** Judging   or   **P** Perceiving.
2. Using Figure 7.7, find the headings representing your preferences and refer to the left-hand column labeled "Learning Preferences." Do the learning preferences generally describe you?
3. Refer to the corresponding column "Test-Taking Strategies." Place a check (✔) in the circles next to the strategies that you *do* use *regularly*.
4. Additionally, if you know whether you prefer to learn using visual, auditory, or kinesthetic/tactile means, take note of those test-taking strategies that are labeled accordingly: Visual = [V], Auditory = [A], Tactile/Kinesthetic = [T/K].

| FIGURE **7.7** | *Test-taking strategies and learning preferences.* |

| **LEARNING PREFERENCES*** | **TEST-TAKING STRATEGIES** |

Extraversion

- Prefers action and variety.
- Prefers talking to people when doing mental work.

○ Five to seven days before an exam, *intersperse small blocks of study time* throughout each day.

○ Vary when and where you study. Also, move about often as you study. [T/K]

○ *Study with others,* either in a study group, a review session, or peer tutoring. [A]

○ *Teach others* the material; this will reinforce what you know. [A]

- Wants to know what others expect of her.
- Prefers seeing how others do a task.

○ If the instructor does not offer, ask for *examples* of test questions, including *models* of essay answers. [V]

○ Prepare by doing *practice tests;* use ready-made study guides and end-of-chapter questions.

○ Schedule extra practice in a laboratory setting. [T/K]

- Often acts quickly, sometimes with little reflection.

○ *Carefully* review the test after completing all questions. As you review, read the items to yourself, moving your mouth [A]. Or, move your finger across the page as you go back over each item. [T/K].

vs. Introversion

- Prefers quiet and time to consider things.
- Prefers doing mental work privately.
- Prefers to work alone or with just a few people.

○ Schedule *larger blocks of study time* five to seven days before the exam.

○ Plan to use a study location away from others: free of visual [V] and auditory [A] distractions; with adequate space to spread out and move about, if preferred [T/K].

- Prefers to understand before acting.

○ Do *timed practice tests* to build speed and confidence, especially if you have long exams or essay questions for a course.

○ Before tackling the exam, get an *overview* and plan how much time to spend on each section.

○ Don't dwell on difficult questions—skip them and return to them later.

Continued.   FIGURE **7.7**

LEARNING PREFERENCES*   TEST-TAKING STRATEGIES

Sensing

- Dislikes new problems.
- Prefers familiar experiences and routines.

○ Find out *early* what type of exam the instructor gives, and set up a study routine accordingly.

○ Establish a time, place, and method of studying that suits you and *keep with it. Write down* when/where/how you will study. As you complete a study session, check it off your schedule. [V] [T/K]

○ Seek out *examples* of test questions, including models of essay answers, case studies, and complicated problems. [V]

○ Ask the instructor for old tests for students' use.

○ Create your own practice tests with similar types of questions.

- Pays more attention to experience and what something *is.*
- Patient with details; impatient with complicated details.

○ Essay tests and word problems can be your weakness; PRACTICE these.

○ Learn how to tackle long, complicated multiple-choice items, including how to eliminate options and take educated guesses. *Practice* until these questions become increasingly familiar to you. [T/K]

○ Go to the instructor, review sessions, or peer tutoring for step-by-step feedback regarding how to answer questions and solve problems likely to be on a test. [A]

vs. Intuition

- Likes solving new problems.
- Likes opportunities for self-instruction individually or with a group.

○ Develop practice tests for yourself and/or for others in a study/review group. [A]

○ Have others quiz you. [A]

- Doesn't mind complicated situations.
- Pays attention to meanings and associations.

○ Create idea maps or diagrams as test review guides. [V]

- Relies on insight more than careful observation.
- Dislikes doing same thing over and over again.

○ Be cautious and take your time when taking a test.

○ After finishing a test, go back and review your answers, looking for careless errors. Carefully go over answers by moving your mouth and "saying" each word [A], or by moving your fingers from word to word [T/K].

FIGURE **7.7** *Continued.*

LEARNING PREFERENCES*	TEST-TAKING STRATEGIES

Thinking

- May hurt others' feelings with-out realizing it.
- Gives more attention to ideas and things, as opposed to human relationships.
- Wants to bring logical order out of confusing situations.

○ If studying with friends, study with "thinking types" like yourself. [A]

○ If you need help from others, seek someone removed from your social circle, such as a professor, peer tutor, or graduate student. [A]

○ Develop review sheets that organize and categorize information, such as a time line, chart, or graph. [V]

vs. Feeling

- Prefers harmony; unsettled by conflict.
- Likes to please other people.
- Can predict how others feel.
- Is very aware of others' feel-ings.
- Learns through personal rela-tionships, rather than impersonal, individualized activ-ities.
- Values appreciation and praise from others.

○ Studying with others in a small group is helpful *only* if everyone in the group gets along with one another. [A]

○ Do not allow yourself to be distracted by others' problems or demands.

○ If needed, isolate yourself away from friends and family members in order to study effectively.

○ Surround yourself with people who are supportive of your aca-demic endeavors.

○ Become a regular, contributing member of a small study group or peer-tutoring group. [A]

Judging

- Prefers to have a settled plan, making decisions ahead of time.
- Prefers a clear structure from the beginning; wants to be able to predict how things will come out.
- Has mind made up; may decide things too quickly, overlooking new or unplanned things.

○ Be conscientious about planning how to best study for a test. Know as much about the test as possible, develop a written time plan, and decide what to study and how to review. [V]

○ Get an *overview* of the test before starting: (1) read (use your eyes and mouth) the directions thoroughly; (2) note the number, type, and point value of questions; and (3) develop a strategy for tack-ling the test within designated time constraints. [V] [A]

○ After finishing, always *go back* through the test a second or third time. Lip-read each item [A] or move your finger from word to word [T/K].

○ When taking the test, you may get anxious because items are not what you expected. Therefore, learn and practice anxiety-reduc-tion techniques beforehand.

Continued.

FIGURE **7.7**

LEARNING PREFERENCES*	TEST-TAKING STRATEGIES

vs. Perceiving

- Studying when surges of impulsive energy come.

  ○ Be aware of your tendency to study for an exam only "when you feel like it." Instead, five to seven days before the exam, plan to add extra daily study time. Allow yourself the freedom of deciding daily *when* you want to study, but *do* study!

- May decide things too slowly.

  ○ *Practice* how to choose the best answer for true/false and multiple-choice items: be aware of wording of test items, how to eliminate and identify choices, and how to take educated guesses.

- Deals easily with unplanned and unexpected happenings.

  ○ This trait could work in your favor in reducing test anxiety. If a test is not as you expected, allow yourself to be surprised; continue with the test, using your flexibility.

- Readily makes changes to deal with unexpected problems.

  ○ If you come across difficult items, skip them, but *be sure* to return to them later.

Key [V]   = Visual
     [A]   = Auditory
     [T/K] = Tactile/Kinesthetic

Source: Learning preferences material from *People Types and Tiger Stripes,* 3rd edition, by Gordon D. Lawrence. Center for Applications of Psychological Type, Gainesville, FL, 1993. Used with permission. This exercise is NOT a type indicator, nor does it replicate the Myers-Briggs Type Indicator® which is a validated instrument.

try it out!

Identify a specific strategy that you will try for an upcoming exam in another class. Using Figure 7.8, write a Personal Action Statement for the strategy. After taking the test, **Assess Your Success:**

- Did you follow through and reward yourself accordingly?
- Did the hurdle materialize, and did you manage it effectively?
- What other changes do you want to make before your next quiz or exam?

FIGURE **7.8** *Your personal action statement.*

Identify an upcoming test: _____

1. I will: _____

    _____

    _____

2. My greatest hurdle to achieving this is: _____

    _____

    _____

3. I will eliminate this hurdle by: _____

    _____

    _____

    _____

4. My time frame for achieving this is: _____

    _____

5. My reward for achieving this is: _____

    _____

    _____

Conclusion

 myriad of factors intertwine to produce successful test results. As test time approaches for each subject, review the following questions as a reminder of strategies that will provide you with the advantages associated with successful test results.

1. ARE YOU SUFFICIENTLY PREPARED?

- Have you *kept up* with week-to-week class *work, assignments,* and regular *review?*
- Have you added *extra study time* the *week before* the exam?
- Have you *reviewed* and *consolidated class notes* and *readings* into a study guide?
- Have you *practiced answering test questions?*
- Have you *"taught"* and thoroughly *discussed* the subject matter with others?

2. ARE YOUR TEST WORRY AND ANXIETY AT A MANAGEABLE LEVEL?

- Have you practiced strategies to *reduce your anxiety* in stressful test situations?
- Do you know *how to calm* both your *thoughts* and your *physical reaction* to a test?

3. ARE YOU KNOWLEDGEABLE ABOUT *HOW* TO TAKE TESTS?

- Do you know the *steps* to follow when taking the test?
- Have you practiced identifying *key words* in questions, including terms and qualifying words?
- Have you practiced *how to answer multiple-choice questions,* that is, how to eliminate incorrect options while choosing the best option?
- Have you practiced *writing essays* that correctly and clearly answer the question?

4. HAVE YOU REVIEWED YOUR CORRECTED TEST?

- Do you have a clear understanding of *why* answers are *correct* or *incorrect?*
- Did you discover *why* you made your *errors?*
- Have you considered ways to *better prepare* yourself for the *next test?*

CHAPTER 8

Continuing Your Academic Success

A REVIEW

FOCUS QUESTION

How can I continue to apply, monitor, and change my system of study?

CHAPTER TERM

After reading this chapter, define and provide an example for the following term:

- Personal Action Plan

As outlined in Chapter 1, your success in college depends on a combination of factors: the learning strategies you choose to apply in and out of class, as well as your attitude and commitment to working hard and achieving your goals. The previous chapters provided you with a medley of strategies to build and strengthen your system of study. However, keep in mind that an effective system of study is not constant. Each term you will face a different set of academic assignments, personal demands, and social desires. At that point, do a personal appraisal of what strategies *do* and *do not* work for you. Adjust your study practices as needed to accommodate your varying courses, instructors, and requirements. The following suggestions will help you select and accomplish those adjustments and, as a result, continue on your path of academic success.

try it out!

Your Personal Action Plan

For each major topic in the text, you chose a specific strategy to apply and then assess by means of a Personal Action Statement. The accumulation of your Personal Action Statements provides an overview of what you have put into practice this semester: *what* strategies you have used and *how* successful they have been for you. Now is the time to review your Personal Action Statements with the intent of combining and modifying them to create a global **Personal Action Plan,** an overview of learning behaviors and attitudes that are effective for *you.* Figure 8.1 is a blueprint for your Personal Action Plan. Complete the three columns to create a personal profile of your study system.

   1. **What I Do Well.** Note specific practices that have become a vital part of your learning and study methods.

   2. **What I Will Change Now.** Jot down a definite approach that likely will benefit you and that you will put into practice. Remember: you are *much more* prone to follow through if you *write down* your intention.

   3. **How Effective?** This column provides a quick means for follow-up. Note how effective or successful you were with the previous change.

My personal action plan.

FIGURE **8.1**

	What I Do Well	What I Will Change Now	How Effective?
1. Managing my time • Use schedule, planner, and calendar. • Balance academic, personal, and social demands. • Reduce procrastination.			
2. Choosing a suitable study location • Minimize distractions. • Organize self, space, and materials.			
3. Selective and attentive listening in class • Create clear, correct, concise notes. • Review notes and create study guides.			
4. Understanding reading assignments • Preview before. • Break up reading. • Create study guides for review.			
5. Using memory tools • Get adequate sleep. • Review immediately. • Study regularly. • Organize/categorize. • Use my senses. • Associate.			

6. Preparing well for tests
• Stay current with work.
• Make review guides.
• Rehearse.
• Manage worry and anxiety.
• Practice reading and answering test items:
  • True/False
  • Multiple Choice
  • Essay			

The following checklist of items was presented in the Conclusion of Chapter 1. Review the checklist, and determine how many of the items you can confidently answer "yes" to. Periodically use the checklist to keep yourself on the track to academic success.

1. Are you clear about *why* you are attending college and *what you expect* to get out of college?

2. Do you know what each instructor *expects of you?* Have you *read*—and reread—each syllabus and met with the instructor? Have you regularly attended review sessions?

3. Are you managing your time *wisely?* Are you periodically assessing your priorities and establishing a routine that balances your academic, personal, and social/leisure demands?

4. Are you *using* effective methods of study for *each* course?

5. Are you *involving yourself* in college life by participating in campus activities?

6. Are you *avoiding* these hazards?
   - Mishandling of your personal freedom and time.
   - Misuse of alcohol and drugs.
   - Mishandling of your personal health.
   - Mishandling of *your best interests.*

As you periodically monitor and adjust how you study and learn, note the sense of self-confidence and empowerment that accompanies your development as a student and a learner. The skills, attitudes, and self-knowledge that lead you toward success in college also will serve you well *out* of college, as you fulfill your career aspirations and personal goals.

A P P E N D I X

Using the Learning and Study Strategies Inventory (LASSI) with This Book

The Learning and Study Strategies Inventory (LASSI) is a self-report instrument assessing college students' use of and attitudes toward learning and study strategies, as defined by 10 scales, each of which is "primarily related to one of three of the components of strategic learning" (Weinstein & Palmer, 2002, pp. 4–6). The scales are broken down as follows:

1. **Skill**—Information Processing (INP), Selecting Main Ideas (SMI), and Test Strategies (TST).
2. **Will**—Anxiety (ANX), Attitude (ATT), and Motivation (MOT).
3. **Self-regulation**—Concentration (CON), Self-Testing (SFT), Study Aids (STA), and Time Management (TMT).

The carbonless, self-scoring test booklet and the online version are both administered in approximately 30 minutes. For each of the 80 items on the instrument, students indicate whether the statement is:

1. "Not at all typical of me"
2. "Not very typical of me"
3. "Somewhat typical of me"
4. "Fairly typical of me"
5. "Very much typical of me"

Scores for each of the 10 scales are presented as percentiles; students are able to compare their learning practices and attitudes in relation to the normative population of college students.

- Students scoring *below the 50th percentile* on any of the 10 scales need substantial work in that area to "increase their chances of succeeding in a post-secondary setting."

- Students scoring *between the 50th and 75th percentile* need some work in that area "to optimize their academic performance."

- Students scoring *above the 75th percentile* have likely mastered that area and "often do not need to work on the strategies or skills for that scale" (Weinstein & Palmer, 2002, p. 7).

The LASSI is described as both a "diagnostic and prescriptive" instrument focusing on thoughts and behaviors "that relate to successful learning in post-secondary educational settings **and** that can be altered through educational interventions" (Weinstein & Palmer, 2002, p. 4). Since each of the 10 scales of the LASSI correlate with topics presented in *College Study: The Essential Ingredients,* the text is an appropriate and comprehensive tool for implementing a prescriptive curriculum (see Figure A.1). Based on results of the LASSI, students can determine the order and thoroughness for completing the chapters and related text features. Students will want to primarily concentrate on:

- Chapters and features related to scales on which they scored *below the 50th percentile,* followed by:

- Chapters and features related to scales on which they scored *between the 50th and 75th percentile.*

LASSI is published by H&H Publishing. Visit our website www.prenhall.com/success and click on the "Partners" button on the home page to access more information.

LASSI scales corresponding to College Study: The Essential Ingredients. FIGURE **A.1**

LASSI SCALE	WHAT SCALE ASSESSES	TEXT CHAPTERS OR FEATURES
SKILL	**Components of Learning**	
Information Processing INP	Use of imagery, verbal elaborations, and organization strategies to learn and remember.	○ Chap. 4: "Active Listening and Note Taking," p. 49 ○ Chap. 5: "Reading and Studying Textbooks," p. 75 ○ Chap. 6: "Enhancing Your Memory," p. 101 ○ Chap. 7: "Success with Tests," p. 111
Selecting Main Ideas SMI	Skills to distinguish important from less important information.	○ Chap. 4: "Active Listening and Note Taking," p. 49 ○ Chap. 5: "Reading and Studying Textbooks," p. 75
Test Strategies TST	Use of preparation and test-taking strategies.	○ Chap. 7: "Success with Tests," p. 111
WILL	**Components of Learning**	
Anxiety ANX	Amount of worry/tenseness that occurs when approaching academic tasks.	○ Chap. 2: "Managing Your Time," p. 15 ○ Chap. 7: "Success with Tests," p. 111
Attitude ATT	Attitudes, interests, and importance of succeeding in college and doing tasks related to success.	○ Chap. 1: "Creating Academic Success," p. 1 ○ Feature: "Student Voices" (within chapters) ○ Feature: "Try It Out!" (within chapters) ○ Feature: "Personal Action Statement" (within chapters)
Motivation MOT	Self-discipline and perseverance about academic tasks; willingness to accept responsibility.	○ Chap. 1: "Creating Academic Success," p. 1 ○ Feature: "Student Voices" (within chapters) ○ Feature: "Try It Out!" (within chapters) ○ Feature: "Personal Action Statement" (within chapters) ○ Chap. 6: "Enhancing Your Memory," p. 101

FIGURE **A.1** *Continued.*

LASSI SCALE	WHAT SCALE ASSESSES	TEXT CHAPTERS OR FEATURES
SELF-REGULATION	Components of Learning	
Concentration CON	Ability to direct and maintain attention toward academics.	○ Chap. 2: "Managing Your Time," p. 15 ○ Chap. 3: "Controlling Your Study Environment," p. 37 ○ Chap. 4: "Active Listening and Note Taking," p. 49 ○ Chap. 5: "Reading and Studying Textbooks," p. 75 ○ Chap. 6: "Enhancing Your Memory," p. 101 ○ Feature: "Focus Questions" (beginning of chapters)
Self-Testing SFT	Use of reviewing and comprehension-monitoring strategies.	○ Chap. 4: "Active Listening and Note Taking," p. 49 ○ Chap. 5: "Reading and Studying Textbooks," p. 75 ○ Chap. 6: "Enhancing Your Memory," p. 101 ○ Chap. 7: "Success with Tests," p. 111
Study Aids STA	Use of support techniques, materials, and resources to help understanding and remembering.	○ Chap. 4: "Active Listening and Note Taking," p. 49 ○ Chap. 5: "Reading and Studying Textbooks," p. 75 ○ Chap. 6: "Enhancing Your Memory," p. 101 ○ Chap. 7: "Success with Tests," p. 111
Time Management TMT	Use of time management schedules and strategies in the academic setting.	○ Chap. 2: "Managing Your Time," p. 15 ○ Chap. 6: "Enhancing Your Memory," p. 101

REFERENCES

Briggs, K. C., and Myers, I. B. (1998). *Myers-Briggs Type Indicator*®, Form M. Palo Alto, CA: Consulting Psychologists Press, Inc. *Myers-Briggs Type Indicator*® and MBTI® are registered trademarks of Consulting Psychologists Press, Inc., Palo Alto, CA.

Lawrence, G. D. (1993). "Exercise: Thinking About Mental Habits." *People Types and Tiger Stripes*, 3rd ed. Gainesville, FL: Center for Applications of Psychological Type, Inc., pp. 2–4.

Pauk, W. (2001). *How to Study in College*. 7th ed. Boston: Houghton Mifflin, pp. 236–241.

Weinstein, C. E., and Palmer, D. R. (2002). *Learning and Study Strategies Inventory*. 2nd ed. Clearwater, FL: H & H Publishing. Available through "Prentice Hall Online Assessments."

INDEX